ENDORSEMENTS

"Steve embodies what it means to love God and love others. As a gifted storyteller with a unique ability to teach biblical truths in practical ways, Steve has helped me experience God's presence and promises in my life. I have found myself laughing and crying as God has encouraged and convicted me as well as many others in our church community through Steve's writing. I highly recommend this book."

—Rev. Steve Southards
Lead Pastor, Salem Church
Clayton, Ohio

"With the heart of the Father and the tenderness of a friend, Pastor Steve Chiles through the art of storytelling will touch your heart, speak truth in love, cheer you on in your journey of faith, and motivate you through the wisdom of the Scriptures to be the person God created you to be."

—Rev. Brenda Snedden
Lead Pastor, Oil City Church of God
Oil City, Pennsylvania

"Pastor Steve Chiles brings you a compiled and inspirational devotional from the Word of God that reveals God's mind, purpose, and will for you and me. *God's Word for You Today* will fill your mind with faith, your heart with truth, and will delight your soul. It is a must-have in your spiritual journey."

—Rev. Salvador Hernandez
Pastor, Centro Cristiano en Shartel
Oklahoma City
Regional Director, Concilio Sur-Centro

"God's Word for You Today" challenges and encourages me to live out daily the truth of God's Word. Pastor Steve is an anointed word craftsman and effective communicator. His down-to-earth imagery and literary giftedness shine the light of God's Spirit into the dark places of the heart, bringing hope and comfort. You too will be inspired and empowered as you read *God's Word for You Today."*

—Dr. Sheryl White
Author, *Underground Angel*
Development Coordinator, Youth Core Ministries

"Steve Chiles is an able writer. Steve is able to connect the truth of scripture to the everyday experiences we face in life. If you are like me, you will wonder how his devotional writings and reflections are often just what you needed from God's Word on the day you read them. His real-life stories and biblical insights will bless you. I love the way Steve ends each devotion with "That's God's Word for you today," because I think you will discover that it *is* God's Word for you today."

—**Dr. Cliff Sanders**
Chair, School of Ministry
Mid-America Christian University

GOD'S WORD FOR YOU TODAY • VOLUME ONE

A WALK THROUGH GOD'S WORD

GENESIS TO REVELATION
IN 100 DEVOTIONALS

STEVE CHILES

dustjacket

Published by Dust Jacket Press
God's Word for You Today, Volume 1: A Walk Through God's Word —
Genesis to Revelation in 100 Devotionals / Steve Chiles

ISBN (Paperback): 978-1-947671-71-3

Dust Jacket Press
P.O. Box 721243
Oklahoma City, OK 73172
www.dustjacket.com

Cover and interior design: D. E. West / ZAQ Designs & Dust Jacket Creative Services

Printed in the United States of America

dustjacket

w w w . d u s t j a c k e t . c o m

CONTENTS

FOREWORD

In a world full of clutter, chatter, and relentless bombardment of negative and opposing views, I thank God for utilizing Pastor Steve's ability to place the spotlight squarely on God's pure and unadulterated love and guidance for each of us. Much like the little colored spy glass that comes with some of the "seek and find books" that we've looked at with our children, God has utilized Steve's daily devotionals in my life to help me ignore all of the "stuff" that clutters my mind and my world and to focus squarely on God's freeing and empowering truths needed for the day.

As an adjunct professor of adult studies, I find that reading Steve's pragmatic and applicable devotional for the day at the beginning of a night class to adult students (most with families) who have come to class straight from work allows them to detox, recalibrate, and relax in the soothing reality of God's all-consuming love. I can almost sense each of them taking a deep breath as they free their minds to take on the evening's new challenge.

I pray that you too will experience God's perfect love expressed in such a relatable manner in the pages of this book.

– Shirley Roddy, Ph.D.
Founding and former Dean of the College of Adult and Graduate Studies and former Dean of Scholarship and Study Abroad, Mid-America Christian University; Adjunct professor in adult studies, researcher, parishioner, wife, mother, grandmother

INTRODUCTION

I did not set out to write a book. My goal was to help the people in my congregation experience God by spending a few moments reflecting on a verse or two of Scripture. So I started writing daily devotionals that I could send out by email.

That was four years ago. I've been writing them every day since. At the encouragement of a young man from back East, I started posting the devotionals on Facebook so a wider audience could enjoy them. *God's Word for You Today* was born.

The responses I've received to the devotionals have been beyond anything I imagined. Every day I receive emails, texts, or comments on Facebook from someone saying how that day's devotional was "just for them." God has an *amazing* ability to give us just what we need when we need it.

Just this week a woman posted on my Facebook page that she had been planning to end her own life that night. But God directed her to the devotional and He used it to give her the hope and comfort she needed in that very desperate moment. I believe with all my heart that God saw her, heard her, and directed her, just as He did me when I wrote it. That's how awesome God's love is for us. That's how awesome His love is for *you*!

This first *God's Word for You Today* book is designed to take you on a journey through the Bible in one hundred daily reflections. Beginning in Genesis and ending in Revelation, you will discover that God had you on His heart all through history. My prayer is that God will inspire you, challenge you, comfort you, and heal you. But most of all I pray that God will *change* you.

So sit with Him for a few moments each day and let the power of His Word speak to you. Open your heart and allow the God who made you to restore you, renew you, and breathe into you a fresh new breath of life.

And don't be surprised if as you're reading a particular devotional on a given day, it seems to be *exactly* what you need in that moment. It's just God letting you know He hears your prayer before you even speak and that He loves you more than you will ever know. May that love overwhelm you and draw you close to your Father's heart. That's God's Word for you today.

1

BLESSED TO BE A BLESSING!

GENESIS 12:1–4

All the families on earth will be blessed through you.
(Genesis 12:3)

"What's in it for me?" Ever ask that question? Maybe that's why we have a hard time figuring out what God's up to in our lives. We keep thinking it's all about *us.*

But what if it's not? What if God's view of the world doesn't stop with me? What if God is actually concerned about *them*?

When God called Abram to leave his father's homeland and follow Him, there were definitely some perks in it for him. He would be famous, rich and have kids. Oh, well—at least the first two are blessings! But what God was up to with Abram really wasn't about Abram. It was about a *world* He would bless. Through Abram's obedience God would lay a foundation of faith that is still being played out in the lives of people today. Abram's journey had a lot of ups and downs and I'm sure there were days he was wondering why in the world he had left his homeland.

The answer? *Them.* It wasn't about Abram being comfortable or happy or free from struggle. It was about them. There was a world God wanted to change and He needed a vessel. That may be a good reminder for us. When we feel God's leading we often think it's about us. If God is leading me to take this job, I *know* I'm going to be successful! If God is leading me to teach this class, I know all the students are going to love me! If God is leading me to start this ministry, I know it's going to be easy and fun and fulfilling. Me, me, me.

But what if it's about *them*? What if being happy and comfortable and successful isn't the primary item on God's agenda? What if it's about some way God wants to bless *them*? Sometimes you have to decide you're going to follow God, not because you'll be blessed but because you get to do something more sacred. You get to be a part of *the blessing.* You may have to decide that there's something more rewarding than being rich or famous, and yes, even better than having kids. It's being a part of God changing the world.

It may not seem as enticing as being rich and famous—I know. But there is something cool about the fact that your life doesn't have to end with just *you*. Here we are, still talking about Abram a few thousand years later. That might be worth following God for. That's God's Word for you today.

> ***Through Abram's obedience God would
> lay a foundation of faith that is still being played
> out in the lives of people today.***

2

WHEN YOUR MESS BECOMES GOD'S MIRACLE

GENESIS 45:1–8

*And now, do not be distressed and do not be
angry with yourselves for selling me here, because it was
to save lives that God sent me ahead of you.*
(Genesis 45:5 NIV)

Do you know what was at the beginning of time? Chaos. Then God spoke and began to make an incredible something out of a mess of nothing. And then He called it all "good." That's what we find God doing in Joseph's life. Joseph had all these awful things that happened to him: abuse, neglect, oppression—you name it; it happened to him.

So where was God in all this? Working. He was right there in the middle of the chaos with Joseph. He was unseen but ever present. And in the end, despite all that had happened to Joseph, God's hand and His plan were clear. Joseph was exactly where he needed to be and God was about to take the sum of the mess of Joseph's life and make a miracle out it.

That's what God can do for *you*! You may feel that you're in a mess right now. Your life may be filled with all the horrible chaos that Joseph's life had. You may not be able to "see" God anywhere. But trust me—He's there, right there in the middle of your mess. Just beyond what you can see, God is at work. He specializes in chaos, including yours. And if you'll trust Him with it, He'll make something remarkable out of it. What you called "awful" today He can make into something good tomorrow.

So lay it before Him—all the pain, all the failures, all the wounds, all the mess. Yield it to His power, His healing, and His control. If you can trust God with the mess, you might end up seeing what Joseph saw: a miracle. He's been making something out of nothing for a long time now. Let Him into *your* chaos. Believe it or not, God's at His best when we're at our worst. That's God's Word for you today.

> *Just beyond what you can see God is at work.*
> *He specializes in chaos—including yours.*

3

WHEN THE TIDE TURNS AGAINST YOU

EXODUS 1:8–14

*Then a new king, to whom Joseph meant nothing,
came to power in Egypt. . . . So the Egyptians
came to dread the Israelites and worked them ruthlessly.
They made their lives bitter with harsh labor in brick
and mortar and with all kinds of work in the
fields; in all their harsh labor the Egyptians
worked them ruthlessly.*
(Exodus 1:8, 12–14 NIV)

How quickly things changed! No sooner was there a change in the Egyptian administration than everything Joseph did was forgotten. The new king didn't care that God used Joseph to save the entire country. That was then. This is now. From adored to unappreciated—just like that.

Has that ever happened to you? Maybe you worked at a company and were a faithful, productive employee. Then your company got sold and your boss, who loved you, got let go. Then you found yourself working for someone who knew half as much as you but was getting paid twice as much as you—and it seemed their goal in life was to make your job as miserable as possible. Or maybe you served in a church. You were wonderfully engaged in a ministry that was fun and fulfilling alongside a pastor you adored. Then the pastor left. In came the new pastor with their newfangled programs, new ways of doing things, and new "vision" for the church—all of which didn't seem to include you or your ministry.

Situations like these leave us feeling used, betrayed, and angry. And not just angry at the company or the church but also at God! How could He let something like this happen? Doesn't He see? Doesn't He care? Yes, He does. But He doesn't always fix it—at least not the way we want. What we want is for our new boss to get fired, for us to get promoted, and for the company culture that we loved to return. Or we want the new pastor to find a new vision that includes us or get a call from God to go someplace else.

That's not what God usually does, though. What He does is work in *us*—that is, if we'll let Him. God has not forgotten your faithfulness, just as He hadn't forgotten the Israelites in Egypt. Behind the scenes God was preparing to do some of the most amazing miracles and feats of deliverance the world had ever seen. It wasn't going to be the way it used to be. But that didn't mean it wasn't going to be amazing!

Don't let fear or exasperation or bitterness get the best of you. If you've been faithful to God, He'll be faithful to you. You'll discover that regardless of who's running the country or the company or the church—God is still on the throne. He was The One who led the people into Egypt and He would lead them out. You too. That's God's Word for you today.

> *Don't let fear, exasperation,*
> *or bitterness get the best of you. If you've been*
> *faithful to God, He'll be faithful to you.*

4

YOUR FIGHT, HIS POWER
EXODUS 3:11–20

*I know that the king of Egypt will not
let you go unless a mighty hand forces him. So I
will raise my hand and strike the Egyptians,
performing all kinds of miracles among them.
Then at last he will let you go.*
(Exodus 3:19–20)

It's not my job. Say that out loud. Doesn't that feel good? It's a wonderful, freeing feeling when you know what you *are* responsible for and what you're *not*! God had just told Moses to go back to Egypt. He was to walk into the court of the most powerful king on the face of the earth and tell him to let the Hebrews go.

Then God gave Moses the bad news: The king was not going to do it. But rather than tell Moses he had to find a way to make it happen, God simply told him that He Himself would take care of it. *"So I will raise my hand. . . . Then at last he will let you go."* Moses was responsible to give the message, but God was responsible to give the freedom.

We often take our work for God too personally. We think it's our job to convince people they need God. We think it's our job to convince people they need to change their ways, change their attitudes, or change their lives. We often get frustrated when we feel God nudging us to invite our neighbors to church and they don't come. God tells us to witness to someone and they fail to respond. God asks us to teach that class and the students don't seem to be listening. God nudges us to serve people in need and they don't seem to be grateful. He tells us to fill that need and it doesn't seem to make a difference. We try to be "Christian" by being kind to that crabby coworker and they only seem to get crabbier.

It's frustrating. But it's not our job to change people. Our job is to go, but it's God's job to do the changing. Moses's job was to put himself in the fight. But it was the power of God that would deliver the knockout blow.

So much of what we want to see happen in our world and in the people around us are things that we cannot bring to pass. We can engage them, serve them, love them, forgive them, challenge them, and listen to them—but only God can deliver them. So say it again: *It's not my job.* When you finally learn what you are responsible for and what God is responsible for, you'll not only be a lot better at freeing others—you'll also set yourself free! That's God's Word for you today.

Our job is to go,
but it's God's job to do the changing.

5

OUR DAILY BREAD
EXODUS 16:13–19, 35

The Israelites called the food manna.
It was white like coriander seed, and it tasted like
honey wafers. . . . So the people of Israel ate
manna for forty years until they arrived at the
land where they would settle.
(Exodus 16:31, 35)

*O*ne *day at a time.* That's how God fed the people for
forty years. Anything they tried to keep overnight
spoiled. So there was no storing up, no hoarding, and no
stockpiling for some rainy day. The word *manna* means
"What is it?" It was probably like some of my wife's casseroles.
Don't ask—just eat it!

The principle God was teaching was that our walk with Him is *daily.* We trust and He provides—one day at a time. I know that's a bit annoying for us security-seekers. We want the big miracle, the big payout, the big answer, and then *we'll* take it from there.

But that's not how God works. He gives us what we need *as* we need it. Some of the reason for this is that God wants to be sure we never forget who it is who's doing the providing! Remember that short-term memory problem we have? Storing up would only lead us to think we didn't need God. And we *do* need Him!

But it's also about relationship. God wants to relate to us and give us gifts of His grace *every day.* "[His mercies] are new every morning" (Lamentations 3:23 NIV). So we get to experience His patience and forgiveness each day. "Each day he carries us in his arms" (Psalm 68:19). Each day we get to experience His tender care. "Each day the Lord pours his unfailing love upon me" (Psalm 42:8). I get to know that I am loved beyond reason—every single day. God wants to take care of us for sure, but He also wants to walk with us and talk with us every day.

So what is it you need from God today? A hug of His love and the assurance that He's so glad He made you? A touch of His grace for a failure, a sin, or a meltdown? A piece of His Bread of Provision to take care of a need? He's here for you.

He may not give you enough to last a year, a month, or maybe even a week. But He has you covered for *today*.

Maybe that's why when Jesus taught us to pray, a part of the prayer was "Give us this day our daily bread" (Matthew 6:11 KJV)—because He knew that's the only way we can live life and stay connected to God: one day at a time. That's God's Word for you today.

***He gives us what we need as we need it
so we never forget who it is who's doing the providing!***

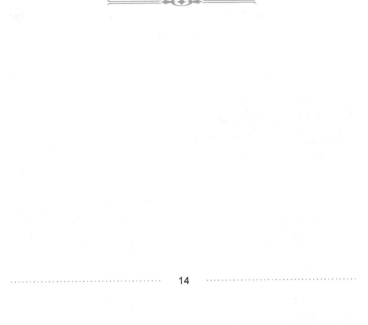

6

A GLIMPSE OF GOLGOTHA
LEVITICUS 9:22–24

*After that, Aaron raised his hands toward
the people and blessed them. Then, after presenting
the sin offering, the burnt offering, and the peace
offering, he stepped down from the altar.*
(Leviticus 9:22)

Many people think of Leviticus as the most boring book in the Bible. Though they have a good case, this passage of Scripture is incredibly exciting! Think about it—it's the very first time for a high priest to offer a sacrifice for the sins of the people. Aaron has to do this perfectly. He follows all the steps, offers all of the sacrifices, and performs the ritual exactly as God had prescribed. Then he steps down, raises his hands with his arms extended outward in the Hebrew form of blessing, and blesses the people.

The first sacrifice. The first high priest. The first atonement of sin for the people. As the people watched, the glory of God came down and the fire of God consumed the sacrifice. It meant God was satisfied. Historic!

But what the people didn't know was they were also getting a glimpse of the future. Generations later the last high priest would offer the last sacrifice for the sins of the people. This sacrifice wouldn't be lambs, bulls, or doves. The high priest Jesus would offer Himself to atone for the sins of people. He stretched out His arms, was nailed to the cross, and blessed the people—all people, everywhere, for all time. His last words were "It is finished." The debt was paid in full. No more sacrifices were needed. God was satisfied. And the glory of God came down upon us all. Historic—and eternal!

Does that leave you in awe? It should. It should remind you that long before you ever thought about your need for God, He was thinking about you! When Aaron stood up and blessed the people, he was blessing you. He was beginning a yearly tradition that would occur every year for 1,500 years until Christ did it once and for all. You were in that crowd of people who needed forgiveness outside the tabernacle. You were among the crowd that stood on the hillside of Golgotha where Jesus was crucified. And you were on the mind of God when He set all of this in motion. So as you go about your day today, take a little of that sense of awe with you. When God gave Aaron the ritual 3,500 years ago, He wasn't thinking just about the people of Israel. He was thinking about *you*. And He hasn't stopped thinking about you since! That's God's Word for you today.

***Long before you ever thought about your need for God, He was thinking about* you.**

7

LIKE FATHER, LIKE SONS
LEVITICUS 19:1–2

The Lord said to Moses,
"Speak to the entire assembly of Israel and say to them:
Be holy because I, the Lord your God, am holy."
(Leviticus 19:1–2 NIV)

Have you ever felt "different"? You are! At least you should be. When God made this statement to His people, that's what He was saying to them. The word *holy* means "separate; set apart." In other words, "I am different from the rest of the world. You be different too." This is significant to understand. God didn't say to the people, "Be religious" *or* "Be legalistic" *or* "Be somber, mean, and judgmental." He said, "Be holy."

Think about all the ways this ought to play out in our lives. In a world that is "every man for himself," we are to be for *others*. God is saying that in a world where everyone wants to see how much they can get, be a *giver*. In a world where people get even, give *grace*. In a world where people are often mean, rude, and selfish, be *kind, polite,* and *generous*. In a world filled with hate, be love.

It's sad that in our generation followers of Christ are most known for what they are against rather than what they are for. Our current political climate has seemingly magnified that image. Don't give in to it. You can stand for your beliefs and speak your views without talking down to others or being rude. You can disagree with other people's views with all your heart without rejecting *them* as people. You don't have to be ugly to be strong and steadfast.

Don't you find it interesting that when God Himself walked on this earth as Jesus Christ, He was known as a "friend of sinners"? In fact, the most violent arguments He had were not with what some might call "the scum of the earth." It was with the most religious. For those religious leaders, holiness was being separate by positioning themselves *above* other people. For Jesus, holiness was being separate by living attractively different *among* others. That's why in Matthew 5 Jesus challenges us by saying that we should have the kind of lives so compelling that everyone will praise our Heavenly Father.

Many think that holiness is a life in which you "do the do's and don't do the don'ts." Avoiding sin is certainly a part of holiness. But it's also about doing what the rest of the world isn't doing and being what the rest of the world isn't being. It's living attractively different in a world that can be ugly and cold.

What would it look like for you to be holy at work today? What's it look like to live a holy life at home, school or at Walmart? Maybe if we stopped trying to be so religious and started trying to be attractively different, we would be a little closer to what God meant when He said this. And maybe others would be a little more interested in the God we serve. That's God's Word for you today.

For Jesus, holiness was being separate by living attractively different **among** *others, not* **above** *them.*

8

THE BLESSING

NUMBERS 6:22–27

"May the Lord bless you and protect you.
May the Lord smile on you and be gracious to you.
May the Lord show you his favor and give you his peace."
(Numbers 6:24–26)

Numbers 6:24–26 is one of the most beautiful passages in the Old Testament. It's the official blessing that God gave to Aaron as His high priest. He was to teach it to the generations of priests who followed him. It's noteworthy for a couple of reasons.

First, it shows the heart of God: "Bless . . . protect . . . smile . . . gracious . . . favor . . . peace." Let those words soak into your soul because they are the words God wants you to hear from Him. He is for you and not against you!

This is what He was talking about when Jesus said that He came that you would have life and "have it to the full" (John 10:10 NIV). God's desire for His people has always been for their good. Notice that God taught the priests to bless, not curse. People don't need God to curse them—they do that to themselves when they reject Him or run from Him.

Second, God wants this to be the constant blessing of the priests over His people. In other words, God wants good stuff, not bad, coming out of mouths of those who are standing in for Him! For those of us who grew up with hellfire-and-brimstone preaching, this is a bit revolutionary. I would have told you as I was growing up that I thought God was mad at me, not glad He made me. Sometimes those of us who are pastors and Christian leaders find ourselves venting our anger and our frustration on our people rather the invoking the blessing of God. Not that we all don't need a swift kick in the pants once in a while, but some of us have made it the theme of our ministry and not the exception.

And here's the real kicker: if you are a Christ follower, you are a priest! God said in Exodus 19:6, "You will be for me a kingdom of priests and a holy nation" (NIV). That idea is brought to fruition in the New Testament.

So my question to you as a priest of God is "What's been coming out of your mouth lately?" Have you been blessing those around you, or have you been cursing them? Does what they hear coming out of your mouth lift them up or bring them down? Being a priest is an awesome responsibility. It's also an awesome opportunity. Those people who annoy you so much?—God loves them. Many of them are the way they are because of stuff you don't even know about. My guess is they need a blessing.

Take a few moments to read that passage over and let it sink into your heart. Let God pour out His heart of blessing on you. Then, like a good priest, take that blessing and pour it out on those in your sphere of influence. And may the smile of God be upon you! That's God's Word for you today.

Being a priest is an awesome responsibility.
It's also an awesome opportunity.

9

WHAT YOU SEE IS WHAT YOU GET!

NUMBERS 13:1–14:25

They will never even see the land I swore to give their ancestors. None of those who have treated me with contempt will ever see it. But my servant Caleb has a different attitude than the others have. He has remained loyal to me, so I will bring him into the land he explored. His descendants will possess their full share of that land.
(Numbers 14:23–24)

"Never let problems blind you to the possibilities." That's a statement worth committing to memory. Here the people were, on the threshold of the promised land. Moses sent twelve spies in to take a look around. The people were waiting on pins and needles to hear about their new home that God had led them to. When the spies returned, ten of them gave the people bad news: "Yes, it's a fertile land, but there are well-fortified cites. The warriors there are huge and legendary. We'll be crushed like insects!"

However, two spies, Joshua and Caleb, gave a different report: "It's a land flowing with milk and honey! Yes, there are large armies there, but we have God on our side! He'll give us victory just as He did before!"

Which spies saw the land accurately? Actually, they all did. The difference was not in what they saw—it was in what they *focused* on! Ten spies focused on the problems. They saw the cities and had no idea how they could scale those walls. They saw the armies and knew they were outnumbered. They saw the warriors and could tell they were outmatched. Problems, problems, problems. The fertile land got minimized—and so did God.

Joshua and Caleb saw the soil, which was rich and fertile. They saw the produce, which was huge and plentiful. They saw the rivers and streams that would water their crops and livestock. And instead of big cities, big armies, and big warriors, they saw *a big God!* Possibilities, possibilities, possibilities! When it was all said and done, only Joshua and Caleb got to go in. All the naysayers and the people who listened to them died in the wilderness. What you see is what you get!

What do *you* see? My guess is that many of us settle for way less than what God wants to do for us, in us, and through us, because all we see are the problems when He wants us to see the possibilities. He wants us to see *Him.* Faith is not the minimizing of life's problems. Rather, it's putting confidence in God's power. It's the belief that He who has led you this far can surely take you all the way to the place He promised. Giants, armies, and walls; crops, cattle, and victory—they are all there before you. Try looking through the eyes of God! That's God's Word for you today.

**The difference was not in what they saw.
It was in what they focused on!**

10

LOVE OR OBEDIENCE?

DEUTERONOMY 6:4–6

You must love the Lord your God with all your heart,
all your soul, and all your strength.
(Deuteronomy 6:5)

Do you love God? I'm not asking if you believe in God. I'm not asking if you go to church, sing Christian songs, say prayers, or give money. I'm not even asking if you are obedient to God. I'm asking if you *love* Him.

Deuteronomy 6:5 is one of the most powerful verses in all of Scripture and one of the most important. Jesus said that it was this verse and one other (about loving your neighbor as yourself) that served as the basis for all the laws and commandments. Simply put, if we would love God wholeheartedly and love others selflessly, we would *do* all the commandments naturally.

But love is so much deeper than compliance or obedience. Love is about vulnerability. It's about intimacy. Obedience and compliance are institutional. Love is personal. When we love God we're not saying prayers—we're talking to our Father. When we love God we're not singing songs—we're expressing emotions, feelings, and affection. When we love God we're not giving money to a cause—we're giving a gift to someone we care about or to something we care about. When we love God we're not going to church—we're setting aside time to spend with Someone who we can't wait to be around. Is that how you went to church this week?

The problem with most of us in our walk with God is not our lack of compliance or obedience. It's our lack of *passion.* We've forgotten who He really is. We've lost touch with what He's done. For many of us it's been a long time since we've thought about how desperately we need Him every day of our lives.

Several years ago I was standing on a stage where I was the guest speaker. The worship leader was leading us in a song I had never heard before, titled "I Will Change Your Name." As we sang it I began sobbing uncontrollably, not in pain but in humble, overwhelming gratitude. The reminder of what God had done in my life left me in awe and love. God had changed *my* name. And my gratitude came bursting out like a geyser. I hope that you are doing your best to be obedient to God. His laws and commands are for your protection and your provision.

But my prayer for you today is that you will fall in love with God again. Sit a while and remember today all He's done for you. Think about how He's given Himself for you. Let Him wash over you again with His grace and presence and touch your heart again. Think about how He's changed your name. Give God your wholehearted love. The other stuff will take care of itself. That's God's Word for you today.

The problem with most of us in our walk with
God is not our lack of compliance or obedience.
It's our lack of **passion.**

11

CHOOSE LIFE!

DEUTERONOMY 30:19–20

Today I have given you the choice between life
and death, between blessings and curses. Now I call
on heaven and earth to witness the choice you make.
Oh, that you would choose life, so that you
and your descendants might live!
(Deuteronomy 30:19)

Every day you hold a nuclear force in your hands. It is a force that can alter your life, the lives of those around you, and the lives of those who come after you. It's a force that can do wonderful and incredible good or horrible and terrible harm. It's the power of choice.

You got up this morning and you chose an attitude. You may not have been aware that you were choosing it, but you did. You chose to be happy, upbeat, and optimistic, or you chose to be grumpy, abrasive, and negative. That choice determined your outlook. It determined how you perceived the things that were said and done to you. Choosing one way gave you the power to expect the best of people, give them the benefit of the doubt, and look for solutions to problems that arose. Choosing the other way caused you to expect the worst from people, find the cloud in every silver lining, and look for someone to blame. And it was all a choice you made.

The importance of today's passage cannot be overstated. God is giving His people final instructions before the promised land is theirs. In this short section He gives them the key to life: choose well. No matter how wonderful the land is before them, it will come to ruin if they don't make the right choices. If they choose correctly they'll keep themselves under the umbrella of His protection and live in the fruitfulness of His provision. If they choose poorly they'll find themselves captives again for generations to come, just as in Egypt, where they started out. You just can't throw this nuclear power of choice around carelessly. The consequences are too great.

Think about the choices before you today. Will you text while you're driving? Will you be optimistic or negative? Will you take time to pray and listen to the voice of God? Who will you spend time with? How will you let them affect you? Will you be kind and caring or will you act like a jerk? Will you be a person of integrity? Will you call that person you had a rift with or will you let that wound bleed one more day?

Choices—think about the power choices have. From car wrecks to healed relationships, it's all in the choices we make. From attractive lives to repulsive ones, from walking with God to walking on our own—it's all in the choices we make. So be careful. God has set before you life and death, blessings and curses. Respect the power that you hold and it will bring you much joy and success and will bless the lives of others. Disrespect it and it will be your undoing.

So choose carefully. Choose wisely. Choose life! That's God's Word for you today.

> *From attractive lives to repulsive ones, from walking with God to walking on our own— it's all in the choices we make.*

12

BE STRONG AND COURAGEOUS!

JOSHUA 1:6–9

This is my command—be strong and courageous!
Do not be afraid or discouraged. For the Lord your
God is with you wherever you go.
(Joshua 1:9)

If there was a message Joshua needed to hear, it was this one: "Be strong and courageous." In the last few chapters of Deuteronomy and the first one of Joshua, he hears it seven times—seven. Moses says it to him. God says it to him. The people say it to him. And he needs to hear it!

He's about to lead about a million people into a new country where they have never been before. He's about to attack incredibly well-fortified cities. He's about fight multiple armies of huge warriors. But those aren't his biggest enemies—

fear and discouragement are. God can help him lead. God can bring down the walls. God can whip the big, bad armies. God can overcome all those obstacles around him. And Joshua has overcome those two enemies within him.

Those two are our biggest enemies as well. Fear paralyzes us. It magnifies the problems and heightens the pain. It makes us see things that aren't there and hear things that aren't meant. Then we run or hide or overreact. That's when we take a tough situation and make it harder. Discouragement is fear's brother. Discouragement happens when we have one setback too many. We're almost out of that hole and then we get hit with that bill we weren't expecting. We thought things were finally getting better with our spouse and then things blow up again. We thought things were finally settled at work and then another round of cutbacks comes and once again we're trying to do more with less. One more pain, one more problem, one more complaint, one more health issue.

Whatever that "one more thing" is, it's the tipping point. Hope drains away and the world begins to seem like a black abyss without a bottom. It's not reality, of course, but it feels that way. That's why fear and discouragement are so powerful. The enemies around you don't have to beat you if the enemies within you do. Many people don't actually lose— they just quit.

But God has not changed. Your "one more" thing still doesn't make your problem bigger than God. Not your one more bill, not your one more marital problem, and not your one more problem at work. God is still with you and for you—and He is still able to see you through it all. Your problem is not really the one in front of you. It's within you. Don't give in to fear and discouragement. You beat them, and then God will take care of the rest. Be strong and courageous—the victory is yours! That's God's Word for you today.

Many people don't actually lose—they just quit.

13

KEEP WALKING

JOSHUA 6:1–20

When the people heard the sound of the
rams' horns, they shouted as loud as they could.
Suddenly, the walls of Jericho collapsed, and the Israelites
charged straight into the town and captured it.
(Joshua 6:20)

Sometimes God answers prayers right away. Sometimes He takes His time. We don't know why. What I do know is that He calls us to stay the course and be persistent in prayer until the answer comes.

In Luke 18 Jesus tells a parable about a relentless widow who just wouldn't quit. It is introduced with "Then Jesus told his disciples a parable to show them that they should always pray and not give up" (Luke 18:1 NIV). We often waste way too much time wondering what God's up to rather than simply doing what Jesus says, to pray and not give up.

In our passage today we're reminded that Joshua and the people were asked to walk around Jericho one time a day for six days. Then on the seventh day they were to walk around it seven times. Why? Some theologians have suggested that the seven times represent God's creation of the world and that He was creating a new world for them here in the promised land. Others have suggested that seven is the "perfect" number and that it represents that this was the work of God, not men. Still others, more pragmatic, have suggested that God used the pounding feet over the course of seven days to loosen the walls to cause them to collapse. Bottom line: no one knows. God said, *Walk,* so they walked.

Did some people wonder why God was having them do this? Probably so. Did others think it was not going to work? Most likely. Did still others think it was an outright dumb thing to do? No doubt. But they walked anyway. Then on the seventh day after the seventh time, the walls came tumbling down.

What is it that you have been praying for? Have you heard God say no? If not, don't quit! I know it may not make sense to you, and you might never come to know exactly why God is taking so long to answer. But before you quit, throw your hands up in despair, and decide God just doesn't answer prayer the way He used to—walk a while longer. Take another lap and trust another day. It may be that it's never going to happen and that God is just using this time to shape you and teach you resilience and patience. Then again, you may find yourself praying one more day and then it happens—out of nowhere the walls come down, your prayer is answered, and the victory is yours!

So take a deep breath, remember again what you know God has told you, and do what many just aren't willing to do: keep walking. That's God's Word for you today.

Before you quit, throw your hands up in despair, and decide God just doesn't answer prayer the way He used to—walk a while longer.

14

IT'S NOT ABOUT YOU

JUDGES 6:11–16

*"But Lord," Gideon replied, "how can I rescue
Israel? My clan is the weakest in the whole tribe
of Manasseh, and I am the least in my entire family!"
The Lord said to him, "I will be with you.
And you will destroy the Midianites as if you
were fighting against one man."*
(Judges 6:15–16)

One of the biggest mistakes we make is to think that
God chooses us for His work because of who *we*
are or what *we* can do. He doesn't. He chooses us because of
who *He* is! For reasons we don't fully understand, He reaches
out from time to time and asks someone who doesn't appear
capable of doing much of anything to do something amazing.

Gideon is a case in point. When the angel of God told him that God wanted to use him to defeat the Midianites, Gideon thought it must a joke. He was a nobody from a nobody family in a whole nobody tribe. Surely there was a mistake. But it was no joke. The problem was that Gideon thought this calling was about *him*. It wasn't. It was about The One who was calling him. Gideon might have been a nobody, but he was being called by a *Somebody*. And that Somebody can use *anybody* to do incredible things.

Don't miss the key sentence in this passage. It's the one that changes everything: *"I will be with you."* Let those words sink deeply into your soul. Regardless of who is on the receiving end of that sentence, when it is God who speaks it, it makes everything possible.

Keep that in mind this week. As you lean into and listen to God and He asks something of you that seems way over your head, remember that it's not about you. Gideon was hiding in a winepress fearing for his life—not the kind of stuff you would think heroes are made of. But when God is with you, it becomes about what *He* is made of!

When God is with us, shepherds become kings, fishermen become apostles, and guys like Gideon become leaders of a revolution. And if God can do that with them, just think what He might be able to do with *you*! That's God's Word for you today.

One of the biggest mistakes we make is to think that God chooses us for His work because of who we are or what we can do. He doesn't.

15

FAILURE ISN'T FINAL

JUDGES 16:22–31

Then Samson prayed to the Lord, "Sovereign Lord, remember me again. O God, please strengthen me just one more time."
(Judges 16:28)

*F*ailure isn't final. I need you to say that out loud. I need you to look in the mirror and say it again. And then say it again. You need to say it over and over until your heart begins to believe it. Because one thing I know about you is that you have failed. In fact, if you live any length of time after reading this, I'm fairly certain you will fail again. You don't mean to, of course. But you most likely will. What you always have to remember is that it's not the end of your story. At least it doesn't have to be.

Samson's story could have easily ended in humiliation. Delilah cut his hair, the Philistines gouged out his eyes, and his strength was gone along with his pride. He was a shell of the man he used to be. He had gone from the most feared man in that region to the joke of the town, from a crusader to a clown.

The Philistines had made a critical error. They didn't know that God does some of His best work out the broken mess of His people. So when the Philistines brought him out to mock him, Samson was a different man, a humbler man. As they put him in the middle for all to laugh at, Samson did something he should have done long before: he turned back to God. With the great grace of God came a great opportunity. Samson remembered why God had called him: to defeat the enemies of God. So he asked God to let him die with one last victory. And God honored his request.

Don't miss the punch line in this story: "So he killed more people when he died than he had during his entire lifetime" (Judges 16:30). Let the full weight of that sink in. God used Samson more mightily *after* he failed than He had before!

Failure isn't final. At least when we let it humble our hearts it's not. God's grace is great enough not only to forgive the past, but He can also use it as preparation for the future. It's not that God *wants* us to fail, because He doesn't. Neither does He want us to wallow in our failure. God would have received no glory from Samson hiding in a cell feeling sorry for himself about how bad he had blown it. He receives no glory when we do the same. But He receives much glory when we allow His grace to heal, renew, and restore us. So get up, humble your heart before God, and move forward. Who knows? Maybe out of the ashes of your failure God will do some of His best work—in your life. Failure isn't final. In fact, sometimes failure is simply a painful stepping-stone to an incredible future. That's God's Word for you today.

> *God used Samson more mightily*
> **after** *he failed than He had before!*

16

THE TREASURE OF A REAL FRIEND

RUTH 1:1–18

But Ruth replied, "Don't ask me to leave you and turn back. Wherever you go, I will go; wherever you live, I will live. Your people will be my people, and your God will be my God. Wherever you die, I will die, and there I will be buried. May the Lord punish me severely if I allow anything but death to separate us!"
(Ruth 1:16–17)

I have nearly five thousand friends on Facebook. They're not really "friends" though—not most of them at least. Many are people I've never actually met who have connected with me through other people. My guess is that you have many of these as well. But certainly there are several who really are friends. Those are people with whom you've shared experiences and have deep connections. Some of them you don't see for long periods of time, but when you do, you pick up right where you left off. They care about the things going on in your life, and you care about them and the things going on in theirs. When you talk there is wonderful laughter and meaningful conversations.

But there are also those friends who are "soul mates." These are people you know are deeply committed to you and are deeply connected to you. They celebrate with you when times are great, and they grieve with you when times are tough. When you talk you sometimes finish each other's sentences. At other times no conversation is even needed for understanding to take place. We usually don't have many of these kinds of friends. We're blessed if we have *one*. Some of us may not have any at all. It's a shame if we don't, because these kinds of friends do more than take away the "aloneness" we sometimes experience. They also remind us of God.

Ruth reminded Naomi by her friendship that she was not alone. Even though Naomi had been through some difficult places, she was still loved and valued by Ruth and by God. She was not cursed, and she was not abandoned. God was with her in her good times, and He would be with her in the bad.

If you have a good friend in the flesh like Ruth, cherish them and cherish the friendship you share. But remember:

you *do* have one in God. No matter what you've gone through, He's there. When you feel you're not worthy of Him, He says you *are*. He will go where you go and stay where you stay. He will stick with you all the way to death and beyond.

Wherever you go today God will go with you. Whatever you do, He is right there beside you. If you do great, He'll cheer. If you blow it, He'll be there for you. Speak His name anywhere you are, and He'll come running to help you. He'll do more than just finish your sentences. He'll answer some of your prayers before you even ask. He's not just a friend—He's your soul mate. That's God's Word for you today.

Wherever you go today God will go with you.

17

AN OLD SOFTIE

1 SAMUEL 1:1–20

*Hannah was in deep anguish, crying bitterly
as she prayed to the Lord. . . . The Lord remembered her
plea, and in due time she gave birth to a son. She named
him Samuel, for she said, "I asked the Lord for him."*
(1 Samuel 1:10; 19–20)

I have to confess something to you. I'm an old softie. If someone makes it into my office asking for help, especially if they're shedding tears, and if I have the ability to help them, I usually do. It just seems God has wired me to be easily moved. I think I get it honestly from my Father.

There are several accounts in scripture when God was responsive to people who were emotional when coming to Him in prayer. Maybe it's because most prayers He hears are just people moving their lips while their hearts are a million miles away. Maybe it's that when people are praying with emotion they are praying with their whole hearts and not just their brains. Or maybe it's that God is a Father whose heart breaks when His children's hearts break. Whatever the reason, one thing is certain: Passionate prayers move the heart of God.

Hannah's story is a good example. She wanted to have a baby—she *really* wanted to have a baby. Unless you have gone through the struggles of infertility, this may be hard to identify with. When you want to have a baby and can't, babies seem to be all you hear about and see. Every friend who announces she is pregnant becomes a dagger in your heart. It's not that you are not happy for her—you are. You're just hurting for *you*!

Hannah's situation was made even more unbearable by her husband's other wife, who threw her ability to bear children in her face! Nice lady—not to mention her husband's tendency to minimize her pain with his "Aren't I enough?" comments.

She came to the temple at the end of her rope and cried out to God as only the most broken of souls would. And God heard and answered her prayer. Her heart was healed, her loneliness removed, and her feelings of worthlessness forgotten. Something amazing happened: her tears touched God, and God touched her.

What's on your heart today? What is it that is so heavy upon you that you can't talk to God about it without the tears beginning to flow? Offer those tears to God. You're special to Him. He made you. You are His child. When He sees your tears, it touches Him. It makes Him want to run to you and sweep you up in His arms.

So don't hold back. Bear your broken places before God. Let your heart cry out with the anguish of Hannah and maybe you'll experience a miracle as she did. Hannah named her baby "Samuel," which means "heard by God." God will hear you too! That's God's Word for you today.

Passionate prayers move the heart of God.

18

IT'S ALL HANDICAPPED SEATING

2 SAMUEL 9:1–13

And Mephibosheth lived in Jerusalem, because he always ate at the king's table; he was lame in both feet.
(2 Samuel 9:13 NIV)

This is one of the most beautiful stories in the Bible. David, wanting to keep the memory of his good friend Jonathan alive, decided to do something good for the family of Saul, Jonathan's father. But after all the wars, he was not sure if there were any relatives still alive. He discovered that there was one. His name was Mephibosheth, a young man who was lame in both feet.

Such people were generally treated only a little better than animals in David's day. They usually had to beg for food or live off the good graces of family. David broke all protocol by doing something unthinkable. He invited this lame grandson of his worst enemy to come be a permanent guest at his table. Not at the servants table, or even a guest table—Mephibosheth was to sit at the table of the king!

You have that same invitation. God invites *you* to come and dine with Him. I know you don't feel worthy. Neither do I. But He doesn't invite us because we are worthy. He invites us out of His love and grace. You may be dirty, stained with the failures and sins from struggling on this fallen planet. You may be permanently scarred by places you've been and things you've done. You may be almost paralyzed by fear, rejection, abandonment, or betrayal. You may feel as if there is no place where you are welcome, where you are wanted—and certainly no place that you could ever be the guest of honor.

But you're wrong. God has a seat for you. Not a seat in the back room, or in the servant's quarters, or even at some side table for visitors—He invites you to sit down with Him: the King of Kings and Lord of Lords. You are His special guest. He has summoned you here Himself.

Oh, by the way, you may feel a little self-conscious sitting there. I'm sure Mephibosheth did. I mean, he didn't deserve to be there. But actually none of the guests did! All of them were there only because the king had invited them. The same is true for all of us. None of us deserve to sit with the King. We've all been stained and fallen and dirty. It's only by

His grace that any of us have a place. And you know what else? We're all handicapped. We all bring a different form of brokenness to the table. We're all defective, from the least to the greatest.

So come to the table of God. Enjoy His presence and His blessing. He loves you and is thrilled you accepted His invitation to be here. And take any seat you want. There are no guests any better than the others. It's all handicapped seating at the table of the King. And we're all welcome! That's God's Word for you today.

We've all been stained and fallen and dirty.
It's only by His grace that any of us have a place.

19

IT'S NOT IN THE GENES— IT'S IN THE CHOICES
1 KINGS 15:9–34

*Asa did what was pleasing in the Lord's sight,
as his ancestor David had done. . . .
Nadab son of Jeroboam began to rule over Israel
in the second year of King Asa's reign in Judah.
He reigned in Israel two years. But he did what
was evil in the Lord's sight and followed the
example of his father, continuing the sins that
Jeroboam had led Israel to commit.*
(1 Kings 15:11, 25–26)

A common theme is found throughout the stories of the kings, especially the evil ones. It's found in the line "and [he] followed the example of his father." The father sinned against God. Then so did the son, then the grandson, and so on. You know the clichés: "Like father, like son," "The apple doesn't fall far from the tree," and "He gets it honest." It was like a generational curse, each one making the same mistakes and committing the same sins that his father did and suffering the same consequences.

But then there's Asa. He *didn't* commit the sins of his father. He decided to reach back a few more generations and model his life after David, "a man after God's own heart." Why? Who knows? Maybe he saw the results of his father's sins and was smart enough to say, "That's not for me!" Maybe he had a mother who was godly or maybe it was his grandmother Maacah. Perhaps somewhere along the way he heard that "still, small voice" of God and knew who it was and followed it. However he learned about the right way, one thing is for sure: He chose it. In spite of how his father had lived, he chose a different path.

And so can *you*! Our parents and our growing-up influences are powerful—that's for sure. But the good news is that we're not slaves to our genes regarding our behavior. We get to choose it. I want to encourage you with this today. If you have addictions, abuse, or dysfunctional behavior in your family of origin, you don't have to repeat it. You can break the chains of those generational curses and start a new chain of generational blessings. If you came from a family where faith wasn't important, or it was lip service only and following God was not practiced much, you can do what Asa did. You can let someone else be your faith model and can start a generational string of those who follow the Lord!

You may not be able to do much about your baldness, predisposition to heart problems, or eye color. That stuff is in your DNA. But you do get to choose how you will follow God. You don't have to be one more statistic of a hand-me-down legacy of messed-up lives. You can start a *new* legacy. Choose it for you. Choose it for those who will come after you. Choose God! That's God's Word for you today.

You can break the chains of those generational curses and start a new chain of generational blessings.

20

KEEP LOOKING!

2 KINGS 6:8–20

Elisha prayed, "Open his eyes, Lord,
so that he may see." Then the Lord opened the
servant's eyes, and he looked and saw the hills full of
horses and chariots of fire all around Elisha.
(2 Kings 6:17 NIV)

I love those 3-D art pieces. You know—the kind you have to stare at for a while for the image to come into view. Each one looks like a mess of colors and lines and shapes at first glance. But if you stare deeply into it, a 3-D image comes into view. I've found that some of them come into view quickly. Others seem to take longer.

It's the same in our walk with God. God is *always* there. Sometimes we see Him clearly. We see Him working, we see

Him moving, we see exactly what He's up to. At other times, however, He's harder to make out. Some of us may feel as if we've never really seen Him. But He's there—just beyond the blur of colors and shapes and lines and images of life coming at us. And every once in a while, just when we think He's nowhere to be found in this mess we're facing—boom! There He is! He didn't just magically appear. He wasn't hiding or teasing or trying to scare us. He was there all along—we just couldn't see Him.

That's what happened for Elisha's servant that day. When he came out to get water from the well, he saw the Aramean army all around them. He was terrified! Then Elisha asked God to open his servant's eyes. When God did, the servant saw the army of God surrounding the Arameans! The difference between the servant's panic and Elisha's peace was in what they *saw*. The servant saw the problem. Elisha saw God. Same mess. Same circumstances. Different image. Sometimes you just have to keep looking.

Got your own 3-D problem you're dealing with today? Are you facing something that looks like a mess and you can't see God anywhere near? Keep looking. They tell you to look *through* the image in a 3-D drawing if you want to see the image. It's the same with God. Maybe your problem isn't really the problem. Maybe your problem is that you just need to see that God already has the problem surrounded. That's usually the difference between panic and peace. Elisha prayed for his servant. How about if I pray for you?

> *Father, I lift up to You today this one who needs to see. Their eyes are filled with all the problems and struggles and confusion that are in front of them. And they need to see You. Lord, reveal Yourself to this precious child. Help them to see Your Power, Your Hand, and Your Purposes at work. Help them to see through whatever they are facing until the image of all that You are becomes clear. Relieve their fears and panic. Fill their heart with Your Peace. Help this child of Yours in every circumstance of life to keep looking—until they see You. In Christ's name. Amen.*

That's God's Word for you today.

> **The difference was in what they saw.**
> **The servant saw the problem. Elisha saw God.**

21

IT'S ALL HIS

1 CHRONICLES 29:10–20

But who am I, and who are my people,
that we could give anything to you? Everything
we have has come from you, and we give you
only what you first gave us!
(1 Chronicles 29:14)

Have you ever thought about how funny it is when young kids want to give gifts to their parents? They hear about the upcoming holiday and they want to get a gift. Problem is, they're *kids.* They don't have any money or even any way of getting to the store. So they ask you to take them. They don't know what kind of gift to get, so you give them affordable ideas about what that gift might be. You help them pick it out and take it to the counter where you pull out your credit card or cash and pay for the gift. You then take it home and get out the wrapping paper and cut, wrap, and tape the gift for them. You then give them a card and they scratch out their own names.

In the whole gift-giving process, signing their names is virtually all they do on their own. But they are so excited to give it. And even though you did it all and paid for it all, you love them for it! Only later, when they're more mature, do they understand. The idea, the transportation, the money, the wrapping—it was all *you*.

That's the childlike view that David is taking in his prayer in today's scripture. He realizes that he has been given a blessed and historic opportunity to raise money for the building of the temple. But he also realizes that everything they are going to use to do it with already belongs to God! It's His trees they'll use for lumber. It's His precious metals they'll use for the sacred items. It's His rocks they'll shape into stones. It's the money He has blessed them with that they'll donate. It's God who is providing the air, the energy, the strength, and even the mental capacity to know how to design such a temple. There will eventually be a beautiful building there and they'll all look at it with pride and say to themselves, "Look at that! Look what we did!" But David knows. It wasn't them—it was *God*. It was all Him.

Are you aware of that? Your life, your health, your mind, your skills—they're all His. These eyes you see with? He made them. Those taste buds that are enjoying that morning coffee while you read this? He created those. Those friends, that job, those kids, that sunset, the fragrance of that flower—they're all His. So when you do something good for God, like dropping in an extra buck into the offering plate or helping teach that class or serving in that ministry, keep that in mind and remember David's words. What you're really giving Him already belongs to Him. We're just children giving gifts back to a Father who provided them all in the first place.

But give them anyway. Because God and parents are both moved by thoughtful and loving kids. It blesses them—even when they're the ones footing the bill! That's God's Word for you today.

We're just children giving gifts back to a Father who provided them all in the first place.

22

JUST TURN AROUND

2 CHRONICLES 7:12–22

Then if my people who are called by my name
will humble themselves and pray and seek my face and
turn from their wicked ways, I will hear from heaven
and will forgive their sins and restore their land.
(2 Chronicles 7:14)

In a message I once told a story about two Russian ships that collided in the Black Sea in 1986. One, the *Admiral Nakhimov,* was an ocean liner carrying 1,234 people. The other was a freighter. The freighter crashed into the side of *Admiral Nakhimov,* causing it to sink in fifteen minutes. It sank so fast that the lifeboats couldn't be deployed. Over four hundred lives were lost. What was so disturbing about the incident was that both captains knew for forty-five minutes that they were on a collision course, but both refused to change direction! Their arrogance and stubbornness had tragic consequences.

Sometimes that's how we get. So intent on doing life our way, we plow ahead. Even when we know the track we're on is not a good one, we often refuse to change course. Unhealthy habits, dangerous behavior, toxic attitudes—we've probably seen the warning signs, but we ignored them. At other times our course is simply one that's not taking us where we want our lives to go. Travel long enough and far enough and we begin to believe it's the only route we *can* take.

But it's not. God has another course for us—a better course, a more fulfilling course, a course that leads to a destiny rather than destruction. Our verse today is one my favorites. It reminds us that God allows U-turns. He tells the people in this passage that they are safe only as they stay close to Him. If they venture off on their own and chase after other "gods," they are putting themselves in harm's way. But if they will humble themselves, call out to Him, and follow His course, He will forgive them and redirect their lives.

Did you hear how easy that was? Admit you're off course, ask God for help, and He'll forgive and restore. Just turn around! You don't have to keep going on the path you're on. With His help you can began a brand-new journey today!

Need course adjustment in your life? Are you happy with the track you're on, or could you use a change? Take a moment and simply tell God you're lost or confused. Admit to Him that you need His help. Ask Him to help you chart a new course with your life. Ask Him to show you the way you need to go. Then follow it!

And do you know what's unbelievable? No matter how long your life has been off course or how far from where you need to be you find yourself, God will bring you back. That's His promise. Pride is sometimes a hard thing to swallow. But it's surely a lot better than an impending shipwreck or a journey leading nowhere.

Just turn around. Set sail with God. The most beautiful part of your journey is still ahead! That's God's Word for you today.

No matter how long your life has been off course,
God will bring you back.

23

HE'S WORKING
EZRA 1:1–11

In the first year of King Cyrus of Persia, t
he Lord fulfilled the prophecy he had
given through Jeremiah. He stirred the
heart of Cyrus to put this proclamation in
writing and to send it throughout his kingdom:
"This is what King Cyrus of Persia says:
'The Lord, the God of heaven, has given me
all the kingdoms of the earth. He has appointed me to
build him a Temple at Jerusalem, which is in Judah.
Any of you who are his people may go to Jerusalem in
Judah to rebuild this Temple of the Lord,
the God of Israel, who lives in Jerusalem.
And may your God be with you!'"
(Ezra 1:1–3)

People often wonder what I do all day. They see me preach on Sunday and show up at funerals, weddings, and the occasional hospital visit, but that's it. I think they assume I just sit at my desk and wait for them to stop by or call me. But I don't. I work. There are sermons to write, events to plan, people to connect with, staff to meet with, books to read, prayers to pray, and devotionals to write. People in my church don't know that even when they can't see me, I'm working. And I'm working for *them*!

The sermons and devotionals I'm writing are hopefully going to help them hear something that will help them. The events I'm planning are for them. I'm helping my staff so they can help them too. So what do I do between Sundays? Believe it or not, I'm working.

So is God, though He sometimes seems hidden. In difficult times, when we can't see God, do you ever wonder what He's doing? He's working. In fact, He's working hard! God was working on Cyrus, king of Persia. Cyrus was not a Jew. He was the king of a foreign country that had conquered Babylon, the king of the country that had taken God's people into captivity. Cyrus had no personal connection to these exiled Israelites, but God moved on his heart until he agreed to let many of the exiles go back and rebuild their temple, which was so sacred to them.

The people of God thought God was gone. He wasn't. Then they thought they were forgotten. They weren't. Where was God then? Working. Just beyond what they could see or understand, God was moving on the heart of a pagan king on their behalf. Not only had He never left them, He also had never stopped working for their good. Because that's the kind of God He is.

If you're in one of those moments when God seems to be taking an awfully long time to act, you may be wondering what He's doing. He's working. And my guess is that He's working hard for you! He's making a way. He's opening a door. He's preparing a place. He's building a bridge. And He's doing it all for you.

Before you know it, the exile will be over and that which you never thought possible will come into reality. Then you'll know. Though you thought God had forgotten you, He hadn't. He was working. That's God's Word for you today.

Though you thought God had forgotten you,
He hadn't. He was working.

24

NEVER-ENDING PROBLEMS, NEVER-ENDING GOD
NEHEMIAH 6:1–16

They were all trying to frighten us, thinking,
"Their hands will get too weak for the work, and it will
not be completed." But I prayed, "Now strengthen my
hands."... So the wall was completed on the twenty-fifth
of Elul, in fifty-two days. When all our enemies heard
about this, all the surrounding nations were afraid and
lost their self-confidence, because they realized that this
work had been done with the help of our God.
(Nehemiah 6:9; 15–16 NIV)

"When it rains, it pours." Isn't that the truth? Sometimes it seems that the problems never end. The car gets fixed, and then the washer breaks down. One child gets well, and then the other gets sick. One crisis gets resolved at work, and another comes right behind it. On and on it goes. When does it end? Never.

I know—I just made your day with that word of encouragement, didn't I? But it's true. Problems are like a never-ending parade in life. They just keep on coming. They may look different from time to time, but they're still problems. There are money problems, health problems, *money* problems, marriage problems, even more *money* problems, kid problems, people problems, work problems, and did I mention more *money* problems? If you're like me, you keep waiting for God to make it stop. But He doesn't. Instead, He just keeps showing up to help us with them. Problems keep us leaning into Him.

Nehemiah got that. From the moment he started the project of rebuilding Jerusalem's walls, the problems started coming—wave after wave after wave. In one last-ditch effort to thwart his work, his enemies were coming after him again. They wanted to discourage, intimidate, and frighten him into giving up. I would have prayed, "Lord, make them stop!" But not Nehemiah. He prayed, *"Now strengthen my hands."* God had given him strength from the very beginning. He had been there for Nehemiah at every turn and for every problem. And even though Nehemiah was discovering that the problems were never-ending, he made a remarkable discovery about God: God was never-ending too!

So if your problems keep coming day after day, take heart. And remember Nehemiah. Problems are never going to end. They will keep coming in all kinds of forms until the moment you take your last breath. But God is as never-ending as the problems you're facing. He was there when you faced the problems before, and He is here as you face your problems today. He is the eternal God, the everlasting God, the never-ending God.

Stop fretting, stop worrying, and stop panicking. The God who saw you through the problems before will see you through again. Pray Nehemiah's prayer: *"Now strengthen my hands."* And may our never-ending God be your strength today and always! That's God's Word for you today.

God is as never-ending as the problems you're facing.

25

TWO MOVES AHEAD

ESTHER 1:1–22

*So if it please the king, we suggest that you
issue a written decree, a law of the Persians and
Medes that cannot be revoked. It should order that
Queen Vashti be forever banished from the presence
of King Xerxes, and that the king should choose
another queen more worthy than she.*
(Esther 1:19)

Have you ever played chess? If you have, you know
that what separates the average player from the
really good player is the ability to see what's coming. The
average player looks at the board and makes what they believe
is their best move. The good player is looking beyond that
move to how the opponent might respond and also how they

will respond to whatever the opponent does. Good players are two moves ahead.

That's how God works. He not only sees what is—He also sees what's coming. That's why He is able to work so effectively on our behalf. We're worried about "what is." He has "what is" covered. He also has "what's next" covered as well. That's what makes Him God. He's two moves ahead.

The opening story in the book of Esther is a good example. The Israelites under King Xerxes's rule are in jeopardy. They just don't know it yet. The king doesn't know it either. But God does. There's a really bad man named Haman who is going to become a lead official under Xerxes. And he's going to come up with a plot to wipe out the Jews in the land. The people of God are going to need an advocate who can speak to Xerxes for them. But who?

That's where God comes in. As Xerxes disposes of his queen, who is being disrespectful of him, it opens the door for a new queen to take her place. And God has just the woman. Her name is Esther. God is going to use her to save an entire race of people. And He is setting it all up before the need even arises. Haman was as conniving as they come. He was crafty and dangerously deceptive in every way. But God was two moves ahead. Checkmate.

That thing you're dealing with today? God saw it coming. He didn't wake up surprised or scared or startled. Before it even came to be, He was on it. He's been moving pieces into place that you weren't even aware of. So don't be afraid. Don't panic. Don't let today's struggle overwhelm you or make you despondent or afraid. God knew what would be on that X-ray scan. He saw that problem coming before it ever hit your desk. That relational shocker that just rocked your world? Yes, He saw that too. You and I can breathe a lot more easily when it comes to this chess game we call "life," because even though it blindsides us sometimes, it never blindsides God.

So put the full weight of your worries today upon the One who's in charge of the game. He's no novice. He's The Grandmaster at this thing. He had your back before you even knew your back needed to be covered. He's two moves ahead. That's God's Word for you today.

God not only sees what is—He also sees what's coming.

26

JUST LET IT GO

ESTHER 3:1–15

When Haman saw that Mordecai would not bow down or show him respect, he was filled with rage. He had learned of Mordecai's nationality, so he decided it was not enough to lay hands on Mordecai alone. Instead, he looked for a way to destroy all the Jews throughout the entire empire of Xerxes.
(**Esther 3:5–6**)

Haman got a promotion. He was now the head of all the nobles. The king had said that people were to bow to Haman to show their respect. But Mordecai didn't We're not sure why. Maybe he knew what we all found out shortly: Haman was a jerk. Most likely it was because, as a Jew, Mordecai reserved bowing for the king and God alone.

But whatever the reason, it ticked Haman off. In fact, it ticked him off so much that Haman wanted revenge. And not just revenge against Mordecai—Haman wanted *all* Jews dead. One little nick of his pride, and Haman was ready to commit genocide. A little over the top, I'd say.

But never underestimate what someone's willing to do in the name of pride. Haman was about to unleash all kinds of pain and suffering—and he himself was going to suffer worse than anyone! Sad. And all he had to do was just let it go. Anger is a seed just looking for a heart to grow in. But the fruit of that anger poisons the one growing it.

I imagine that as some of us woke up this morning, the first thing on our minds was something someone said or did that offended us recently. We've been fuming about it—if not outwardly, then inwardly. We're giving someone the "silent treatment." We're answering questions with sharp responses or making little snide, sarcastic remarks. We're telling several other people about our "injustice." Some of us may even be thinking about a way that we're going to get even. But there is no "even." The pain we inflict never quite satisfies. And most of the time *we* end up suffering the worst.

So just let it go. Give the anger no place to set down roots, and I promise you: it'll go away. Feed it and you have no idea where it may end. When that knucklehead cuts you off in traffic, or when that clerk is curt and short with you, or when you hear that a coworker said something mean about you, just let it go. You know who you are. They're only words.

Please hear my heart. I'm not saying there's not a time to confront things in our relationships or our interactions with others. I'm just saying it's not every time. If it's like Haman and it's just your pride getting nicked a bit, then just let it go. Attacking or reacting will just make a bad moment worse. Your pride will heal, and you will have performed a sacred act called "giving grace." You never know—you might need a bit of that yourself one day soon! That's God's Word for you today.

> *Anger is a seed just looking for a heart*
> *to grow in. Just let it go.*

27

WHEN IT ALL COMES CRASHING DOWN

JOB 1:13–22

Job stood up and tore his robe in grief.
Then he shaved his head and fell to the ground to
worship. He said, "I came naked from my mother's
womb, and I will be naked when I leave. The Lord
gave me what I had, and the Lord has taken
it away. Praise the name of the Lord!" In all of this,
Job did not sin by blaming God.
(Job 1:20–22)

One of my favorite old hymns is the song "It Is Well with My Soul." The first verse says, "When peace like a river attendeth my way, / When sorrows like sea billows roll, / Whatever my lot, Thou hast taught me to say, / 'It is well, it is well with my soul.'"

These were not words penned from a great imagination. They were written with the ink of a broken heart by a man whose world had just come crashing down. Horatio G. Spafford was an attorney and investor. But most of the property in which he had invested burned in the great Chicago fire. His four-year-old son died from scarlet fever. When he sent his wife and four daughters to England for a holiday, the ship they were on was hit by another vessel, and 226 people lost their lives. Spafford's four daughters were among them. On his journey to join his wife, who had survived, he wrote the song. A man of lesser faith would have turned his back on God. But not Spafford. He turned *to* God. That was the only thing that kept him going.

Long before Spafford, there was Job. His is also a story of great faith. Job had a great life. He had land, livestock, wealth, servants, and family. But then it all came crashing down. Piece by piece, Job lost everything he had, including his health. His wife encouraged him to "curse God and die." Nothing like having an empathetic spouse behind you!

But though Job had lost nearly everything, he refused to let go of the one thing that held it all together: his faith in God. He knew that life was filled with both triumph and tragedy. And he resolved that he would stay faithful to God in both. If you read through the book of Job, you'll hear him process his grief, his pain, and his frustration. But though he wrestled with God, he didn't give up on Him. With his world crashing down, he would need God's help to put it back together!

Maybe you've been through a "world-crashing" experience recently. Maybe you've felt like a distant cousin to both Horatio and Job. Maybe you've been wondering what in the world you've done to deserve such pain and sorrow. The answer? Nothing. Triumph and tragedy are a part of everyone's journey. Some of us just get more than our fair share.

But don't turn *from* God. Turn *to* Him. The one you praised in the blessings is the one who is with you in the pain. Lean into Him and let Him put His loving arms around you. Wrestle with Him if you must, but don't let go of Him. Draw from His strength and rest in His peace. Even if it feels that your world is crashing down around you, it can still be well with your soul. That's God's Word for you today.

> *The one you praised in the blessings is the one who is with you in the pain.*

28

THE HEALING POWER OF JUST BEING THERE
JOB 2:11–13

*Then they sat on the ground with him for seven days
and nights. No one said a word to Job, for they saw that
his suffering was too great for words.*
(Job 2:13)

Have you ever been in a situation with someone who is hurting and you didn't know what to say? What if I told you that most of the time you're better off saying little to nothing at all? In most tragedies your words are the least helpful thing you can bring. What's needed most is your presence. When you show up, people know you care. Your tears help them cry. Your nearness helps them feel safe. Your hugs help them feel your love. Your *being there* has incredible, healing power.

Your presence helps remove the greatest enemy of those experiencing tragedy: aloneness. Being alone magnifies fear and amplifies pain. Just being there reduces those. Your presence doesn't make all the pain go away, but it does make it bearable. And you don't have to even say a word.

I know it feels awkward. We want to say something. It's almost as if we believe that the "right words" will be like a magical incantation that will lift the grief from their hearts and give them a perspective that will change how they feel. But there are no such words. Tears are a gift that God gave us to get the hurt out, and grieving takes time.

What most people need are simply others who care enough to stay near without having to say much at all—just a simple "I'm so sorry" or I love you." In all the situations I've seen as a pastor, the people who are most helpful are those who simply remain attentive and close. Perhaps putting a hand on the person's shoulder when they're sobbing, or fetching some water, a cough drop, or a cup of coffee. Those are little things. But they mean so much.

So don't worry if you have a friend or family member going through a difficult time and you just don't have the words to say. Your words really aren't needed. *You* are needed. Job's friends gave him an incredible gift. They simply sat with him for seven straight days. The scripture doesn't say, but I'm going to guess that they got some water for him and maybe some bread. He was covered with sores so they probably couldn't hug him, but I feel sure they did what they could to help.

What they *didn't* do, at least for seven days, was talk. They were simply *there*. And that, I promise you, meant the world to Job. So when you hear of someone you care about who's suffering, go. Just show up, be attentive, and say as little as possible. There will be time for words later. It's the healing power of your presence that the person needs right now. Just *be there*. That's God's Word for you today.

> *What most people need are simply others who care enough to stay near without having to say much at all.*

29

CLOSER THAN YOU THINK

PSALM 34

*The Lord hears his people when they
call to him for help. He rescues them from all
their troubles. The Lord is close to the brokenhearted;
he rescues those whose spirits are crushed.*
(Psalm 34:17–18)

Tom McCay and his wife, Maggie, were on a flight from Atlanta to Houston. A retired Air Force pilot, Tom said he always fantasized about a pilot having a medical emergency and his having to save the day by stepping into the cockpit and flying the plane to safety.

But on this particular flight it was Tom who had the medical emergency. About thirty minutes before starting the descent into Houston, Tom started feeling ill and slipped into a semi-conscious state. He became cold, sweaty, and unresponsive. Maggie became hysterical, pushed the call button for a flight attendant, and began screaming, "Are there any medical personnel on board?" You can imagine how startled she was when about twenty people sitting in the areas behind her all said in unison, "Yes!" A group of doctors from Houston, who had attended a medical conference in Atlanta, were on the flight returning home.

Tom was quickly laid across the seats, and two of the doctors worked him, getting him stabilized. Tom was taken to a hospital upon landing and recovered just fine. In reflection, Maggie said, "I was crying, 'He is my world—please help him! Please help him!' I just feel that God was hovering over that plane." He was. Even at thirty thousand feet, God is closer than you think.

You may need to know that today. As you head into that difficult meeting, God is close. As you have that painful conversation, God is close. As you make those heartbreaking decisions about what to do with your aging parents, God is close. As you sit with your checkbook and that overwhelming stack of bills, God is close.

Actually, He's not just close—He's closer than you know! He knew about that meeting and that conversation long before you did. He saw this day with your parents coming years ago and not one of those bills has caught Him by surprise. When

Maggie and Tom were on that plane, those doctors were there all along. Maggie and Tom just didn't *know* they were there until Maggie cried out for help.

It's the same with God. You may not be aware of Him, but He's right there. Though you can't always see Him or even sense Him at times, He's there. When you call, He hears. When you need help, He rescues. No matter where you are or what you are going through, God is near. He has resources you are not aware of and answers you have not thought of. Even at thirty thousand feet—God is closer than you think. That's God's Word for you today.

> **No matter where you are or what you are going through, God is near.**

30

HE IS WHAT YOU'RE LOOKING FOR!

PSALM 37

Take delight in the Lord,
and he will give you your heart's desires.
(Psalm 37:4)

A few common themes are found among lottery winners. One, those who didn't manage their money well when they had only a little don't manage it well when they have a lot. Two, lottery winners discover relatives that they never knew they had coming out of the woodwork and calling them! And three, most of the time the winners are not happier after winning the lottery. In fact, most end up feeling worse about life.

Jack Whittaker, one of the largest lottery winners ever, clearing $315 million dollars, ended up miserable and bankrupt. He stated, "I wish I had torn up the ticket."

Loneliness and isolation are common among lottery winners. So is depression. So is suicide. Meanwhile, millions of people keep playing, hoping they can strike it rich too. They have no idea that if they're not happy now they most likely won't be happy regardless of how rich they become! Money and all it can buy isn't really what our souls are looking for. *God* is what we're looking for.

That's the point David makes in Psalm 37. He tells us to stop envying people who are chasing after money or positions or power. It's not making them nearly as happy as we think. In the middle of this discourse he says, *Take delight in the Lord, and he will give you your heart's desires.* Take a good look at this verse. It doesn't say that if you really follow God that He is going to give you everything you want. This is important because it's how many people interpret this verse. They think, "God's going to give me the desires of my heart, and I really desire that new car, so I know He's going to give it to me!" Wrong. God is not going to give you what your *greed* desires. God is going to give you what your *heart* desires.

What your heart desires is *love,* and *God* is love. What your heart desires is peace, and *Jesus* is our Prince of Peace. What your heart desires is to be made complete, and *God alone* is the one who completes us. God's not going to give you what you think you're looking for. He *is* what you're looking for! *God* is the desire of your heart!

So when the next lottery winner makes the news, don't turn green with envy. When your coworker gets that promotion, don't curse them. When you see someone who has something you really, really want, remember: If you don't already have what you need in your heart, nothing else you reach for will satisfy. If you have God, you already have what your heart desires. Open your heart fully to Him and you'll come to realize that for yourself. Give yourself fully to God today—not because He's going to give you what you're looking for, but because *He is* what you're looking for! That's God's Word for you today.

> *God is not going to give you what your **greed** desires but what your **heart** desires.*

31

OVERCOMING SPIRITUAL SPATIAL DISORIENTATION

Trust in the Lord with all your heart; do not depend on your own understanding. Seek his will in all you do, and he will show you which path to take.
(Proverbs 3:5–6)

I was reading an interesting article recently on "spatial disorientation." It's a condition that can affect pilots, particularly when they are flying in the clouds. Because they can't see past the front of the plane, they can't tell if the "attitude" of the plane is where it's supposed to be or not, that is, if the plane is orientated properly with the horizon. Their balance can get off, and their inner ears, which control balance, will adjust to what they think it should be. Sometimes pilots will be veering to the right or left and not even know it. They can be slowly spiraling down toward the ground and be totally unaware—all because their senses are telling them that it "feels" right.

The really interesting thing is that most planes contain the instruments to let the pilot know whether the plane has the proper attitude or not. The problem is that some pilots are so convinced that their senses are correct, they will ignore what the instruments say and stay on their course! If they don't come out of the clouds soon enough or trust their instruments quickly enough and right the plane, they crash. Spatial disorientation is a major contributor to plane accidents.

Our Proverbs passage today reminds us that the same thing can happen to us on our life journey. "Trust in the Lord with all your heart; do not depend on your own understanding." That's hard to do, isn't it? We see the way we think things ought to go and we pursue that way, even when God may be saying something different to us. It may "feel right" or "seem right." It might be something other people are affirming as well. But our verse today tells us not to trust those things. God has a way, a plan, and a will for us that are best.

Following our own plans, ideas, and desires can lead us to crash and burn. We need to have the faith to push back on ourselves when our way is off course from what God is saying. His way is the right way—no matter what our own minds may be telling us.

So where are you headed this week? Are you "on course" with the flight plan that God has for you? Maybe you've been lost in the clouds for a while and find yourself somewhat confused or disoriented. It would be a good idea to look to Him and *"seek His will in all you do."* God loves you, and you can trust Him. He will show you the path you are to take. Don't be a victim of spiritual spatial disorientation. Don't keep going on the path you're on if you know it's different from what God is saying.

Adjust your life to His Path, His Way, and His Plan. Let Him adjust the "attitude" of your life to fit His Horizon for you. I promise you: even though your way *seems* right, God's way *is* right! You can trust Him to get you safely to where you need to be. That's God's Word for you today.

**We see the way we think things ought to go
and we pursue that way, even when God may be
saying something different to us.**

32

EAGLES OR TURKEYS?

Walk with the wise and become wise;
associate with fools and get in trouble.
(Proverbs 13:20)

On December 14, 2013, a sixteen-year-old named Clifton was with a group of his friends in the San Francisco area when one of them came up with an idea: "Let's rob somebody!" They went to a housing complex about 11 PM and saw a man walking alone. They surrounded him and one of the members of the group pulled a gun and demanded the man hand over all his valuables. The man complied without resistance.

But the teen, for whatever reason, decided to shoot the man anyway. The bullet glanced off the man's face, only wounding him. However, the bullet then struck Clifton in the head, killing him instantly. His "friends" all ran away and left him with the victim. Another sixteen-year-old was eventually arrested and charged with robbery and murder. Clifton wasn't the one doing the shooting. Nor was he the one being robbed. He was simply at the wrong place at the wrong time and with the wrong group of people. And it cost him his life.

If I could give young people only one gift, it would be the gift to choose their friends carefully Our friends help shape our character, our attitude, our values, and our behavior. And most of the time we're not even aware of it! We "adjust" ourselves to fit in. We compromise ourselves to be accepted. We change who we are and sometimes forfeit who we want to become just to blend in with "the herd." The people we surround ourselves with have a powerful impact on who we become and what we achieve—for good or for bad!

Sometimes, like Clifton, our friends impact us in ways we would never anticipate. Most of us, as we look back across our lives, can identify the "wise" people who made us better than we could have ever been by ourselves. We can also identify "fools" we hung out with who caused us great grief. Who we chose to be close to helped determine in many ways what we went through and ultimately who we became. And it's still that way.

So who are you hanging out with? Spend enough time around negative people, and you'll begin to grow negative. Hang out with people who talk badly about other people, and soon you'll be joining in the gossip. But hang around people who are positive, uplifting, and encouraging, and after a while you'll feel better about life and its possibilities! Spend time around people who are caring, compassionate, and kind, and you'll become that way too.

Think about people you know who seem wise and thoughtful and have a godly perspective on life. Hang out with those people. Like it or not, you'll tend to become like the people you let close to you. So choose carefully. It's hard to soar with the eagles if you spend all your time with a bunch of turkeys. That's God's Word for you today.

Our friends help shape our character, our attitude, our values, and our behavior.

33

QUIT FLYING SOLO!

*Two people are better off than one, for they
can help each other succeed. If one person falls, the
other can reach out and help. But someone who falls
alone is in real trouble. Likewise, two people lying close
together can keep each other warm. But how can one be
warm alone? A person standing alone can be attacked
and defeated, but two can stand back-to-back and
conquer. Three are even better, for a triple-braided
cord is not easily broken.*
(Ecclesiastes 4:9–12)

Stop it. Stop trying to do life all by yourself. It's dumb.
And it's selfish. It's dumb because often the answer to
the problem you're wrestling may be in the hands or mind of
someone fairly near to you.

I had three different conversations this week with people whose problems and struggles could have been solved easily and quickly if they had just reached out to someone close to them. In all three scenarios, someone near to them could've helped immensely. But all three decided to go it on their own. They ended up lonely, frustrated, and defeated. All three agreed after the fact that going it alone is a dumb thing to do.

Doing life by all by yourself is also selfish. When you fly solo, you not only rob yourself of the benefit of those who can help you, but you also remove yourself from those who need *your* help! You may have the answer that someone is looking for. You may be the help that someone needs. You may be the one who could make their day so much better by simply being in a position in which they could reach out to you. Don't do life alone. If they crash and burn, or try and fail and cry alone, you are to blame. God put you on this planet for them, just as He put them on this planet for you!

"The Teacher" of Ecclesiastes reminds us of God's observation at the beginning of creation: *"It's not good to be alone."* Listen to the Teacher again: *"Two people are better off than one."* What a simple but powerful statement! There's support in two. There's protection in two. There's synergy in two. There's comfort and warmth in two. All we need to do is break out of our isolation and quit wallowing in our self-pity, frustration, and struggle. We need to connect. We need to reach out. We need to let another person in. When we do this we become a team, a community, a family. Life is just better when we live that way.

So just stop it. Stop flying solo. Come out of your cave and reconnect. Stop telling yourself all those lies about no one caring or no one really loving you or no one really wanting to know. We *do* want to know. Just as *you* would want to know if it were us. So listen to the Teacher and put his words into practice. Two really are better than one. Oh, yeah—and three are even better! That's God's Word for you today.

Flying solo robs you of the benefit of those who can help you—as well as those who need* your *help!

34

HOPELESSLY IN LOVE

You have captured my heart, my treasure, my bride.
You hold it hostage with one glance of your eyes.
(Song of Solomon 4:9)

Have you ever fallen in love? I mean *hopelessly* in love? So in love that the person who is the object of your affection is all you can think about? So in love that your heart aches when you are not with them? So in love that you would do anything just to be with them? We often think that kind of love is only something for the movies. No one really acts and feels that way. Or do they?

Our verse today is taken from the Song of Solomon. It is easily the most romantic book in the Bible. It is the back-and-forth exchange between a lover and his beloved. There are parts of it that are so personal and private that they'll make you blush. So how did a piece of literature like this make it into the Bible? Because it isn't just about the love between a man and woman. It's about God and how hopelessly in love He is with *you*!

You have captured the heart of God. You hold His heart hostage. He makes it clear over and over again that He cannot get you out of His mind. He is constantly thinking about you. He constantly wants to be with you. Even in your worst moments, when you have rejected His love and have turned away from Him, He can't stop thinking about you. He *never* stops loving you. You are the object of His affection. You know what else? He doesn't want it any other way!

If you woke up today feeling a bit unloved or uncared about, read this verse again out loud. Imagine God smiling at you and extending His arms toward you. It doesn't matter where you've been or what you've been doing. It doesn't matter how long it's been since you've talked with Him or even thought about Him. Even though He's not been on *your* mind, *you've* been on *His*. So lean into Him for a few moments today, and let Him remind you again how much He loves you. He crossed eternity to be with you. He gave His Son to show His love for you. And the greatest thing you can ever do for Him is simply to love Him in return.

I know it doesn't make any sense. But love seldom does. You've stolen His heart. His desire is to steal yours as well! That's God's Word for you today.

> ***You have captured the heart of God.***
> ***You hold His heart hostage.***

35

AN INSURMOUNTABLE DEBT

"Come now, let's settle this," says the Lord.
"Though your sins are like scarlet, I will make them as
white as snow. Though they are red like crimson,
I will make them as white as wool."
(Isaiah 1:18)

On May 28, 1562, a little village in Germany called Mittenwalde lent 400 guilders to the city of Berlin. Berlin never paid it back. Adjusting for inflation, that amount would be about 11,200 guilders or $137 million in today's economy. Add compound interest to that and the debt now is in the trillions of dollars! About every fifty years or so since 1820 the mayors of Mittenwalde have asked Berlin for the debt to be paid. But Berlin, unfortunately, doesn't have that kind of money lying around—or *any* kind of money lying around as they are currently operating in the red. The only way this can be resolved is obviously for Mittenwalde to forgive the debt. But that's an awful lot of forgiveness!

Isaiah's words to Israel fall along those same lines. After all God has done, again and again, Israel has rejected Him and gone their own way. They haven't sinned just once or twice or broken only one or two of God's commands. They've sinned *repeatedly* and broken every commandment God has given. Their debt of sin is insurmountable. There aren't enough animals to sacrifice or grain to offer or prayers to pray. There is no amount of rituals they can perform that can cover even a fraction of a debt like that.

So God offers them freely what they cannot afford to purchase: *forgiveness.* Though they are red with sin, He will make them white with His holiness. What they cannot do for themselves, He will do for them. Debt forgiven.

By the way, that offer from God is one He still makes! What God offered them He offers to *you.* No matter how deep a hole you have dug, He will fill it. No matter how far you have strayed, He will bring you back. No matter what you have done or how many times you have done it or how long you have been in the darkness of sin, God offers His grace, His forgiveness, and His light.

You may struggle with receiving it. You may even struggle with forgiving yourself. But He wants to settle this. He doesn't want you to hide, or run, or try to dodge Him anymore. Though your sins are red as crimson, He will wrap you in His holiness and make you white as wool. *"If we confess our sins, he is faithful and just and will forgive us our sins and purify us from all unrighteousness."* (1 John 1:9 NIV) Your sin may be insurmountable, but it's not unforgivable. You can begin a new journey with God debt free! That's God's Word for you today.

> **Your sin may be insurmountable,**
> **but it's not unforgivable.**

36

HE'S MORE THAN YOU THINK!

ISAIAH 9:6–7

For a child is born to us, a son is given to us.
The government will rest on his shoulders. And he
will be called: Wonderful Counselor, Mighty God,
Everlasting Father, Prince of Peace.
(Isaiah 9:6)

Our passage today is an amazing and important prophecy about the coming of Jesus. Take a look again at these names: *"Wonderful Counselor, Mighty God, Everlasting Father, Prince of Peace."* When the Jews thought of the Messiah, they were mostly thinking about a warrior. They had in mind someone along the lines of King David but better. He would be a fierce and powerful leader who would lead the people out of exile and back into being a great nation.

STEVE CHILES

They were looking for a king who would be courageous, fearless, and commanding. They were looking for a leader who would capture the hearts and minds of the people. But they were mostly looking for just an extraordinary man. What they weren't expecting was God Himself to come!

Jesus was more than just a great charismatic leader. He was more than a healer, a prophet, or a great teacher. He was the *"Wonderful Counselor,"* the One from whom all wisdom comes. He was the *"Mighty God,"* the El Shaddai of old, now in the flesh. He was the *"Everlasting Father,"* the Creator and origin of all that is. He was the *"Prince of Peace,"* the Reconciler who finally restored humanity to a right relationship with God. The people of Israel would have been happy to simply be the greatest nation on earth again. But God had something more in mind. He was going to give them more than they imagined and all they would need. He gave them Himself as the Messiah. And He saved not only Israel—He saved the entire world!

Who do you need Jesus to be to you today? Need wisdom? The *"Wonderful Counselor"* is in and is waiting to advise you. Need power or courage? The *"Mighty God"* stands ready to help. Need comfort or encouragement or a steadying hand? Your *"Everlasting Father"* is right here. Need to be reconciled to God or someone else? He's still the *"Prince of Peace."* God didn't send you just a Messiah. He sent you *Himself.* He is so much more than you can imagine and all you will ever need. For unto you that child was born, and unto you that Son was given. So call upon Him for whatever you need. He has it covered. That's God's Word for you today.

**_God didn't send you just a Messiah.
He sent you Himself._**

37

GRACE BEFORE YOU KNOW YOU NEED IT

A remnant will return; yes, the remnant of
Jacob will return to the Mighty God.
(Isaiah 10:21)

I want you to read this verse carefully. It's one of those verses that would be easy to blow by when you're reading a prophetic book like Isaiah. But I think this is such an amazing insight into the heart and purposes of God. Listen again: *"A remnant will return."* What's so special about that phrase? They haven't even left yet! Isaiah writes these words *before* the people are taken away into captivity. While God could have just pounded away about the stupidity of their sin or how much pain their actions are going to cause them, He says something else. He lets them know that His grace is already in motion. Before their sin had ever reached its peak, before their pride and arrogance had led them to a painful captivity, before the consequences of their sin had even begun, God was planning for their return. That, ladies and gentlemen, is how big God's heart is for His people! It was the promise of grace before they even needed it.

Let me be clear: God doesn't want His people to fail. He doesn't want them to sin. He wants them to love Him, follow Him, and be obedient to Him. He doesn't want them to suffer the consequences of disobedience. He cheers for us to succeed. But the fact of the matter is that our failure doesn't catch Him off guard. God's ready. In fact, He's not only ready for the failure, but He's already preparing a plan to draw us back! That's grace before we even know we need it.

I hope you do great for God today. I hope you are faithful, strong, and obedient. I hope you are a wonderful model to your family and a great example to those you work with or go to school with. I hope you are the spitting image of Jesus Himself in all you do or say.

But if you blow it, don't give up on yourself. God hasn't thrown in the towel on you. And don't you give up on that child or friend or boss who blew it either. They're just like you—flesh-and-blood failures who often manage to lose their way and are in desperate need of the mercy of God. But with you and with them, God's neither surprised nor exasperated.

He's ready. He's ready to forgive. He's ready to restore. He's ready with a second chance. In fact, He'll be heading your way with grace before you know you need it. That's God's Word for you today.

> *Before their sin ever reached its peak,*
> *God was planning for their return.*

38

IT'S ALL ON HIM

ISAIAH 53:3–12

All of us, like sheep, have strayed away.
We have left God's paths to follow our own. Yet
the Lord laid on him the sins of us all.
(Isaiah 53:6)

This is one of the most humbling verses in the Bible for me. I was a sinner, and a proficient one. Yet God, in His divine plan, took all my sins and placed them upon the only One who was ever perfect: Jesus Christ. He didn't have to. He could have allowed me to wallow in my guilt and ultimately pay for my failures. He could have banished me from His presence, struck me down in my rebellion, or let me burn for eternity in hell.

But He didn't. He took every sin I had ever committed and put them upon His only Son. He willingly died as a symbol of His love and as a statement of the finality of my struggle. Gone. I don't have to fear anymore. I don't have to work to prove myself. I don't have to do anything but open my arms to His love. He made me worthy. He made me a Son. He took all my sin and put it on Himself. It's *all* on Him.

Interesting how we like to pay for our own sin, isn't it? We like to believe sometimes that if we can make ourselves feel bad enough that the sin will be removed. Or if we can just do enough good stuff the score will be evened. Or maybe if we can just really, really mean it when we say we'll never fail again.

But none of those things work. The good news is that they don't have to work. God did for us what we couldn't do for ourselves. He lifted our sin from us and put it upon Himself. Only His holiness could overcome our worldliness. Only His righteousness could overcome our sinfulness. Only His faithfulness could overcome our continuous failure. As Isaiah said, we really are just like sheep that go astray. But our Shepherd's arms of love can reach us no matter where we go!

So if you've been struggling because you've sinned, failed, or had one more time when you've not lived up to what you said you would be, welcome to the flock. We are all like sheep that go astray sometimes. But don't run. Don't hide. And don't lie there beating yourself up trying to make yourself feel bad enough so that you'll feel better. Confess to your Shepherd that you've sinned. He already knows. Let Him lift the burden of sin from you. You can't bear the weight of it. But He can. He can take the sin of all of us. And He did. It's *all* on Him! That's God's Word for you today.

> *God did for us what we couldn't*
> *do for ourselves. He lifted our sin from us*
> *and put it upon Himself.*

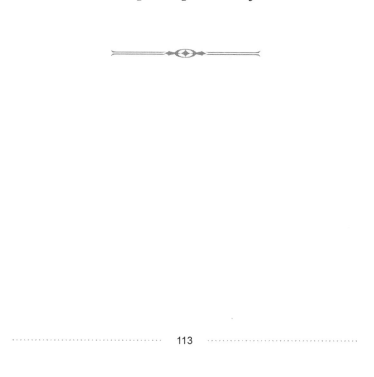

39

AT THE CROSSROADS

This is what the Lord says: "Stop at the crossroads and look around. Ask for the old, godly way, and walk in it. Travel its path, and you will find rest for your souls."
(Jeremiah 6:16)

Stop. Take a look at where you are. Even more import-antly, take a look at where you're going. Is it where you want to go? Do you know where the road you're on is going to take you? If you stay on it, is it making who you want to be? Are you happy with who you've become so far? If not, what are you going to do about it? Most of the time we don't think about what we're doing or what road we're taking. We just go. Where we end up is where we end up, and who we become is who we become. But it doesn't have to be that way—we can choose.

Every day is a crossroads. We can make choices that will take us in whatever direction we want to go. But we have to be thoughtful about those decisions. The road we take is going to take us somewhere, so we might want to think about that *before* we get on it! And if we find ourselves on a road that's wearing us out, exhausting us inside and out, and making us increasingly unhappy with ourselves and what we're doing with our lives, it may be time for a different road.

Jeremiah reminds us that when we get to a thoughtful crossroads in our lives, it's a good time to get back on track with God. God's road is still a good road. It's still a safe road. It's a road that will lead you to peace. Maybe it's time to get back into church. For some of us it's been a while. Maybe it's time we stopped going to some places too. Some of those places just aren't good for us. Maybe it's time to get around some better people, choose a better lifestyle, or spend a little more time reflecting and a little less time running.

It doesn't matter what road you've been on or how long you've been on it. Today is new day. It's a crossroads day. It's a chance to turn your life in a better direction. Maybe it's time to get back to that old godly road you used to know.

God would love to walk with you again. And maybe you'll experience something you haven't experienced in a long, long time—rest for your soul. That's God's Word for you today.

> *The road we take is going to take*
> *us somewhere, so we might want to think*
> *about that* **before** *we get on it!*

40

HAS GOD GOT A PLAN FOR YOU!

"I I know the plans I have for you," declares the
Lord, "plans to prosper you and not to harm you,
plans to give you hope and a future."
(Jeremiah 29:11 NIV)

"God hates me." Ever feel like that? Maybe you had a really bad day or a fairly awful week, or maybe it seems as if you've been being picked on by life for a good while now. Sure, some of it may have been your own mistakes. But how long is this going to last? Is God going to leave me in this mess forever? No. He has plans for you—good plans, plans to prosper you, not to make you miserable. Even if *you* are the cause of your mess, He doesn't want to leave you there. He wants to get you out. He wants to bring you back!

That's the great news behind our verse for today. God is speaking to the people who are in exile because they messed up. They were the ones who walked away, not Him. They were the ones who decided to do life their way instead of His. Now they're suffering for it. Many people would just look at them and say, "You're getting what you deserve!" And that would be true.

But that's the crazy thing about God. Instead of giving us what we deserve, He offers us what we *don't* deserve—another chance, a better way, a different plan. Oh, yes—and there's some other great news too: We don't have to wait until we're in a mess to get in sync with God's plan! God would much rather have us follow Him and discover His will and His way for our lives instead of going off on our own and ending up in some exiled land. We can come to Him *now*. If His plans for us are good when we're at our worst, just think how good they can be when we're at our best!

God has plans for you—good plans, great plans. Whether you're at the top of your game or at the end of your rope, He has plans. He doesn't want you to stay where you are. He wants to bring you out. He wants to bring you back. He wants to take you toward an incredible future that He's prepared just for you. So if your plans aren't working out the way you had hoped, don't despair. Try His. They're good! That's God's Word for you today.

Even if you *are the cause of your mess, God doesn't want to leave you there.*

41

AN EVERYDAY GIFT

LAMENTATIONS 3:19–26

The faithful love of the Lord never ends!
His mercies never cease. Great is his faithfulness;
his mercies begin afresh each morning.
(Lamentations 3:22–23)

One of the great stories from Exodus, when God was leading His people from Egypt to the promised land, is how He fed them: He gave them manna. It was a substance they could use to make bread with.

One of the really cool parts of the story was how God provided it: every day. Every day they could go out and gather all they needed for the day. It wouldn't keep overnight because it would spoil. But it didn't have to keep. God was faithful to have it ready—every single day, all the way to the promised land. They didn't do anything to earn it, and they couldn't work or till the soil to make it. It was a gift of His grace—an everyday gift.

Our verse from Lamentations today reminds us that His grace is still an everyday gift. Did you fail yesterday? Did you fall a bit short of being all you know you should have been? Did you blow it big? It's okay. That's yesterday. This is today. His faithful love doesn't end. There is no bottom to it and there is no top to it. You can't do anything to earn it. You can't work for it and you don't have to beg for it. He freely and willingly offers it—fresh, new, every morning. You can't store it up for future use, but that's okay, because you don't have to. When you wake up tomorrow, He'll be there again. God is as faithful as the sunrise. His mercy is as fresh and wonderful as that freshly baked manna. He will satisfy your hunger for forgiveness and wholeness and peace.

So go ahead—reach out for His mercy today. Taste and see for yourself that the Lord is good. Experience what His people have been experiencing since the days of the Exodus: the everyday gift of God's love and grace. Sit down and let Him serve you. If you're tired, just rest. If you're weary, let Him surround you with His strength. If you find yourself beaten, battered, and defeated today, let Him wash over you with renewal and new life.

Enjoy the manna of God's presence. Discover for yourself how great the faithfulness of God really is. He'll keep offering you the bread of life day after day—all the way to the promised land. That's God's Word for you today.

God will satisfy your hunger for forgiveness and wholeness and peace.

42

CLOSE ENCOUNTERS OF THE *GOD* KIND

All around him was a glowing halo,
like a rainbow shining in the clouds on a rainy day.
This is what the glory of the Lord looked like to me.
When I saw it, I fell face down on the ground, and
I heard someone's voice speaking to me.
(Ezekiel 1:28)

Have you ever encountered God? I mean, have you ever had an experience in which you felt Him, heard Him, or saw Him in a way that was staggering or overwhelming? Ezekiel did. And he was never the same again! It defined his calling as a prophet and made God real to him—very, very real. I've never known anyone who had a moment as dramatic as Ezekiel did, but I have known some who have had some very powerful ones. I had one myself some years back. They are life-altering moments. You are never the same afterward.

My observation about these encounters is that they are God-chosen and not person-chosen, although most of the time they happen when we really *need* to hear from God. One man's story he told me was when he was an agnostic, but he was pleading with God for the life of someone he loved. He wanted some kind of affirmation from God. He picked up a Bible in a hospital waiting room and when he opened it, a passage was literally glowing. It was the words he needed. More importantly, it was an *experience* he needed. God became *real* and *near* to him in that moment. And that man has remained changed ever since.

Another person I know who had no religious background heard God's voice as she was huddled up in a corner of a horse stall. She had been devastated by some recent events in her life and was in great despair. She felt God touch her shoulder and heard Him say to her, "It doesn't have to be this way." Feeling an overwhelming sense of peace, she picked up an old King James Bible and began reading and discovered that God loved her and had a wonderful plan for her life. She was never the same again.

Do you need to hear from God today? If you do, it would be great if He were to speak to you the way he did to Ezekiel or my friends. But even if He's not that dramatic, here's what I can tell you for sure: He *is* speaking to you. God doesn't always have to appear in blinding glory for you to see Him. He doesn't have to make the words in the Bible glow for you to read them. And He doesn't have to speak with such audible clarity that it makes the hairs on the back of your neck stand up. Most God encounters are a lot subtler than that. But if your mind is open and your heart is surrendered, they can be just as life altering.

If you need God, He's there. If you're listening, He'll speak. God wants to work in the lives of everyone, not just the prophets or those of us with dramatic stories. I hope you have a close encounter with God today, one that touches you exactly as you need to be touched. And I hope that afterward you too are never again the same. That's God's Word for you today.

> ***God doesn't always have to appear in blinding glory for you to see Him.***

43

CAN THESE BONES LIVE?

EZEKIEL 37:1–6

"This is what the Sovereign Lord says: Look!
I am going to put breath into you and make you
live again! I will put flesh and muscles on you and
cover you with skin. I will put breath into you, and you
will come to life. Then you will know that I am the Lord."
(Ezekiel 37:5–6)

I was visiting recently with a friend who has just lost his
second wife. To endure one loss of a spouse would be a
terribly traumatic thing. To endure two is simply unthinkable.
You could see in his eyes a weariness, a heaviness, a lifelessness.
He was depleted. He looked lost and a bit bewildered. My
heart broke for him.

I imagine he felt a bit like Ezekiel when God showed him a valley of dry bones and asked, "Can these bones live again?"

"You alone know, Lord" was Ezekiel's response. In other words, "I don't see how that's possible, God. The life is all gone. Is there something you can do?" Yes, there is.

One of God's specialties is bringing life where there is none. He breathed into barren dust at the beginning of time, and humanity was born out of it—not life from life, but life from dust. That may be a message some of us need to hear. You may have been through an experience recently that sucked all the life out of you, maybe a painful loss like what my friend had. Or maybe you've been working with every ounce of energy on a project or a goal, and it's all for naught. You are now standing there with nothing to show for endless hours of effort. Or maybe you've poured everything you've had into a relationship, trying desperately to make it work. And the person still walked away. Now you're empty. You're exhausted. You're spent. Can *these* bones live? Yes, they can.

The same God who breathed life into a lump of clay and named him "Adam" can breathe life into *you.* He can restore your hope, renew your joy, and refill your tank. He will walk with you while you go through your valley of grief and take you all the way to the new road that's on the other side.

Put the full weight of your exhaustion on Him today. Don't hold back. Cry out to Him from the depths of your pain and your sorrow. Let Him into the deep, dark places where you feel as if you have died and let Him breathe His life, His peace, and His comfort into you.

Old dry bones don't always just jump right up. Sometimes it takes a bit for them to all come together. But trust me—the same God who brought a whole valley of dry bones to life can speak to *your* dry bones as well. *"Can these bones live?"* Yes, they can. Ezekiel's did. So can yours! That's God's Word for you today.

> **The same God who breathed life
> into a lump of clay and named him
> "Adam" can breathe life into you.**

44

GIVING CREDIT WHERE CREDIT IS DUE

DANIEL 2

*The king said to Daniel, "Is this true? Can you
tell me what my dream was and what it means?"
Daniel replied, "There are no wise men, enchanters,
magicians, or fortune-tellers who can reveal the
king's secret. But there is a God in heaven who reveals
secrets, and he has shown King Nebuchadnezzar
what will happen in the future."*
(Daniel 2:26–28)

Don't you just love Daniel? When you read these
stories about him, you discover that he was an
extremely gifted, very popular individual. He was one of those
young, talented, good-looking guys whom everybody else
wanted to be like. He had every reason to be proud, arrogant,

and braggadocio. But he wasn't. In fact, what made him so endearing was his pure and humble heart. Today's passage is a great example of that.

King Nebuchadnezzar had experienced a dream that disturbed him. He believed it was from "the gods" and had deep meaning behind it. But he knew that if he told his advisors the dream they would just make something up. So he said he wanted someone who could tell him *what* he dreamed as well as what it meant.

When Daniel heard about it, he prayed, and God revealed both the dream and the meaning to him. So Daniel went to the king with the answer. What happened next revealed the essence of Daniel's character. When the king asked Daniel if he could tell him the dream and the meaning, Daniel said, "No. But God can." Instead of taking the glory and flaunting his knowledge, Daniel gave all the credit back to God. He could have made a big deal out of himself and what he could do. But he didn't. He made a big deal out of *God.* And God blessed him for it.

Do you do that? Are you aware of how many of the gifts, talents, opportunities, and outcomes of your life are from God? Do you give Him credit when you can? It's easy to forget sometimes. When the crowds applaud, when people compliment, when the boss gives us a raise for our good work, sometimes we forget that it's not really about us—it's about

Him. We may not always get the chance to point it back to God in the moment, but we can always thank Him privately.

Maybe today is a good day to do that. Take a moment and think about some of the cool stuff you've been able to do, create, teach, or accomplish. Think about the last really nice compliment you had. Then let God know how grateful you are that He chose you to give those gifts to or bless and use in this way. Let Him know that you are very aware that it's Him, not you.

Like Daniel, let's dare to do great things for God. But let us never forget to give credit where the credit is really due! That's God's Word for you today.

> **When the crowds applaud,**
> **it's not really about us—it's about Him.**

45

GOD IS ABLE!

Shadrach, Meshach, and Abednego replied,
"O Nebuchadnezzar, we do not need to defend ourselves
before you. If we are thrown into the blazing furnace,
the God whom we serve is able to save us. He will
rescue us from your power, Your Majesty."
(Daniel 3:16–17)

You know what God is? He's *able*. He's able to do whatever it is you need Him to do, whenever it is that you need Him to do it. It doesn't matter the circumstances. In Mark 9 a father says to Jesus, "If you can do anything, please help us," to which Jesus responds, "If I can? All things are possible to him who believes." You see, *if* doesn't exist in the vocabulary of God. He is the one who does what needs to be done. It doesn't matter whether it's to heal when the doctors don't know what else to do, to intervene when all other options have been tried, to provide when the resources are all gone, or to protect you when you're helpless and vulnerable. He's able—completely able.

It's that belief that helped the three friends of Daniel stand strong even when threatened by King Nebuchadnezzar himself. They believed that even though the most powerful king in that part of the world was standing in front of them, there was a more powerful King standing with them. So no matter what Nebuchadnezzar said would happen to them, they didn't move. They believed their King was able. He was able to change Nebuchadnezzar's mind. He was able to help them escape. He was able to have someone intervene on their behalf. Or, if need be, He was able to protect them from the flames of the fire. They didn't know *how* God would do it, but they knew He *could*. Their God was able.

God is able for you too. The same God who delivered them can deliver you. He can still change minds, intervene in situations, provide necessary resources, protect you, and heal you. Whatever you need, whenever you need it, God is able. Just reach out to Him today. Don't let whatever is standing in front of you cause you to cower in fear. Don't back down from who you are or who God has called you to be.

Stand up and declare today from the bottom of your being, "My God is able!" Put the full weight of all you're facing upon Him, because He is fully up to the challenge. His power to deliver you is as great as His love is for you. He's not just a "good and faithful" God. He's an able God—completely able. That's God's Word for you today.

His power to deliver you is as great as His love is for you.

46

RIDICULOUSLY LOVED

*When the Lord first began speaking to
Israel through Hosea, he said to him,
"Go and marry a prostitute."*
(Hosea 1:2)

This was not the girl most moms would pick for
their sons. This girl had *baggage*—bad home, bad
decisions, and not exactly on a course for future success. But
God picked Gomer to be the wife of Hosea for a reason. God
wanted to show just how "ridiculous" His love for His people
really was. Even though they were prostituting themselves
with other gods and chasing after everything *but* God, He still
wanted them. Even though they were ridiculously unfaithful
to Him, He would be ridiculously faithful to *them*. Even

though they had a boatload of baggage, He had an ocean full of grace. Even though they had given up on themselves, He would never give up on them. And He still doesn't. Aren't you glad?

I don't know about you, but I realize that I'm not exactly the greatest catch God could come up with. But He loves me anyway. I'm certainly not the most faithful servant He has, but He's relentlessly faithful to me. Even though I have a boatload of issues and problems and baggage, He opens His arms to me with His endless grace. Even when I want to give up on myself, He never does. Hosea's story isn't just about him and Gomer. It's not even just about Israel. It's about me. Believe it or not, it's about you too. And it's a story of a Ridiculous Love.

God thinks you are the pick of the litter, the cream of the crop, the crown jewel. Regardless of where you've been, what you've done, or how deep in the muck and mire of sin and failure you've sunken, He still chooses *you*! It doesn't matter if, like Gomer, you've gone back to that life again and again. It hasn't changed God's love for you one iota. You're still beautiful to Him. You're still precious and priceless and perfect. You're still worth pursuing with all His heart.

You may not think of yourself as "the perfect catch" for anyone's son or daughter. But God thinks you are *exactly* the kind of person He's looking for. I know that sounds crazy, but that's just how God is. So you might was well give in to His love, because He will never, ever give up on you. Because His love for you is just *ridiculous*! That's God's Word for you today.

> ***Regardless of where you've been,***
> ***what you've done, or how deep in the muck and***
> ***mire of sin and failure you've sunken,***
> ***God still chooses* you*!*

47

ANYTHING!

Then, after doing all those things,
I will pour out my Spirit upon all people.
Your sons and daughters will prophesy. Your old
men will dream dreams, and your young men
will see visions. In those days I will pour out my
Spirit even on servants—men and women alike.
(Joel 2:28–29)

You know what you're capable of? Anything. Think about that for a minute. You're not limited because of how old or how young you are. You're not limited because of your gender. You're not limited by your station in life or whether you're wealthy or poor. You're not limited by your intelligence. You're not limited by your family lineage. You're not even limited by your talents and abilities. You see, none of these things, though important, are the deciding factor in what you can do or how far you can go. There is another factor that trumps all of those: the Spirit of God!

Today's passage, from Joel, was quoted by the apostle Peter when he preached on the Day of Pentecost in Acts 2. The people in Jerusalem were amazed because they heard these uneducated fishermen speaking in their native languages, which they knew they couldn't possibly know. God used this moment to show the world that a new day had dawned. The Spirit of God was now going to be made available to *all* people who called upon the name of the Lord. He was the Great Equalizer, the Great Enabler, the Great Equipper.

Now people could find not only forgiveness in their lives but also meaning and purpose too! Joel's prophecy came true: the Spirit of God came, and a group of no-name fishermen rocked the world. The Spirit of God has continued to work through all kinds of people ever since.

So what would God do in and through *you* if you let Him? Let go of the excuses and embrace the power of His Holy Spirit. Stop focusing on what you feel you *can't* do and listen to what God is saying you *can* do. Stop listening to the people who say you're too old or too young. Stop listening to the people who say you can't because you're a woman. Stop listening to all the naysayers who think they know your limits. They don't.

Joel reminds us that God's Spirit has been poured out upon *all* people—and that would include you. So why not begin asking God what the "anything" is that *you* are capable of? Because "anything" is exactly what you can do when the Spirit of God lives in you! That's God's Word for you today.

> ***Stop focusing on what you feel you* can't
> *do and listen to what God is saying you* can *do!***

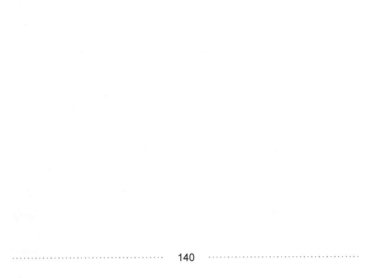

48

INSIDE THE FISH

From inside the fish Jonah prayed
to the Lord his God.
(Jonah 2:1 NIV)

I heard a story some years ago that I love. Two pastors were in a church office together arguing over the best posture for prayer. One said, "I think that my most passionate prayers are prayed when I'm standing on my feet with my arms outstretched toward heaven." The other pastor replied, "I found I'm most passionate when I'm prostrate on the floor with my face buried in the carpet."

While they were debating, a telephone repairman who was working on the office phone lines said, "I think you're both wrong. I find my most passionate prayers have been when

I've lost my footing high up on a telephone pole and I end up dangling upside down thirty feet above the ground with nothing but a wire wrapped around my ankle!"

I think the telephone repairman was right on. Fear and desperation make passionate prayer warriors out of us all. It certainly worked for Jonah. He ran from God for all he was worth until he ended up getting swallowed by a fish. But being inside that fish made him see things differently. He couldn't run anymore. So he did what we all should do in times like that: he cried out to God—and God heard him.

Maybe you're "inside the fish" yourself today. You feel trapped, desperate, out of options, surrounded by darkness. Your future looks bleak. Now might be a good time to pray. In fact, it's in places and times like this that we do our *best* praying! That's because it's "inside the fish" that we realize how much of a mess we make of our lives without God's help. "Inside the fish" we're broken, humble, and teachable. "Inside the fish" is sometimes the place where we finally come to the end of ourselves and our own way of doing things.

Many of us would say that getting our lives on track began with a passionate prayer at a time when we were "inside the fish." That was where God finally had our full and undivided attention. It's sad it has to be that way, but we often don't really "get it" until we're "inside the fish."

So if that's where you are today, I'm sorry. I know it's horribly scary. And yes, it stinks. But God is there—and He is listening. He wants to help.

Now listen very carefully to this part because it's important: God wants you to do more than wanting to *get out.* He wants you to *be different.* He wants you to keep that same broken, humble, teachable spirit once you get out of the mess you're in. If you don't, you'll just end up running again, swimming for your life again, and ending up back in that fish again.

So cry out to God today. With all your heart, soul, mind, and strength, cry out to Him. If you'll learn and take with you what God is teaching you in there, you'll do more than just get out—you'll *stay* out! And one day you'll even thank Him for the great lessons you had to learn "inside the fish." That's God's Word for you today.

> *"Inside the fish" is sometimes the*
> *place where we finally come to the end of*
> *ourselves and our own way of doing things.*

49

NO OTHER GODS LIKE OURS!

*Where is another God like you, who pardons
the guilt of the remnant, overlooking the sins of his
special people? You will not stay angry with your people
forever, because you delight in showing unfailing love.*
(Micah 7:18)

You know one of the reasons I know that the God of the Bible is the *real* God? Because we would never make up a God like this! When Micah asks the question "Where is another God like you?" the obvious answer is *nowhere*. All around the world cultures have created gods in their own image. They are demanding gods. They are unforgiving gods. They are gods that require a child or a virgin as a sacrifice. They are gods who take *much* and give *little*. Those kinds of gods remind you of *people:* fallen, twisted, and self-consumed. People created these gods.

But our God is so much different than that. He's the unexpected and surprising God. He doesn't come demanding—He comes *inviting.* He doesn't come angrily—He comes *gently.* He doesn't hold our sins and failures over our heads—He comes with *forgiveness.* He doesn't come requiring the sacrifice of virgins and children or anything else for that matter. He Himself became The Sacrifice on our behalf.

We could never come up with a story line like that! Our minds don't think that way. Our hearts don't work that way. Our lives aren't lived that way. God is nothing like the way people are when they are in charge. That's why we know that the Lord God is Unique, Special, and Holy. We would never come up with a God like Him. He is the One True God, and there is no other.

Take a moment today just to be in awe as Micah was. The people of Israel were a hot mess of sin and stupidity, but God told them through Micah that He wanted to redeem them anyway. He says that same kind of stuff to *you.* He's not mad at you or holding anything over your head today. He simply comes offering you all His love, all His joy, and all His life. All you have to do is open your heart and life to receive it.

Where is there another God like this? Nowhere—nowhere but *here*, that is. And He's here with you! That's God's Word for you today.

> **When Micah asks the question
> "Where is another God like you?"
> the obvious answer is nowhere.**

50

THE STORM SHELTER

*The Lord is good, a strong refuge when
trouble comes. He is close to those who trust in him.*
(Nahum 1:7)

When we decided to move back to Oklahoma City
my wife insisted we put in a storm shelter when
we bought a house. Oklahoma is a part of "tornado alley,"
and Wanda has a high need for security. I thought it was kind
of a silly expense—it was going cost about $3,000, which was
no small amount with all the other house-buying expenses.
Besides, I reasoned, we had lived in Oklahoma City six
years before without one and never really had much of a
tornado threat.

But she was adamant, so I agreed that once we got everything settled we would have one put in. Six weeks after we had moved into our house, the storm shelter still wasn't in, and we left for our son's college graduation in Portland, Oregon. The night before we returned to Oklahoma one of my new neighbors called and told me a small tornado had come through our neighborhood that afternoon and had torn off about a third of our roof and wiped out several sections of fence.

The storm shelter was put in *immediately* upon our return. And yes, we've been in it several times since. You don't always need a storm shelter, but when you do need one, they are lifesavers—literally *lifesavers!*

Nahum reminds us that God is like that for us. He's there. We're not always overwhelmed by life, but when we are He's there. The bottom doesn't always drop out from under us, but when it does He's there. There are many days when we're able to easily navigate through all the challenges that come our way. But then there are those days when we don't have the strength to navigate at all. On those days He's there.

God is a Guide and an ever-present Friend and Companion *every* day of our lives. He loves those everyday conversations and interactions and the moments we just sit and think about how awesome and wonderful He is. But when the clouds get dark, the wind picks up, and life unleashes its fury upon us,

He's there—not just as a Friend, Guide, and Encourager but also as a Shelter. He will hold us through the storm.

I hope you don't need God like that this week, but if you do He's there. If there's a crisis at work, a disaster at home, or if life just decides to dump more on you than you think you can handle, He's there. He's a Strong Refuge for you. He's a Protective Shelter. He is *close* and He is *mighty*. He will see you through your storm.

As much as I hate to admit it, my wife was right. We needed a shelter a lot more than I thought we would. My guess is that you'll need a shelter from time to time yourself. And when you do, you have One! That's God's Word for you today.

God is there—not just as a Friend, Guide, and Encourager but also as a Shelter.

51

"YOU WOULDN'T BELIEVE IT ANWAY"

The Lord replied, "Look around at the nations;
look and be amazed! For I am doing something
in your own day, something you wouldn't believe
even if someone told you about it."
(Habakkuk 1:5)

On their way home from church a mother asked
her young son what his Sunday School lesson was
about that morning. He told her it was the story of the
Israelites getting out of Egypt. She said, "Well, what did the
teacher say?"

"The teacher told us that first there were bombers that
came in and bombed the Egyptians, so all the Israelites
escaped," he explained. "Then the Egyptians rallied their

troops and started chasing God's people all the way to the Red Sea, where the Israelites built these pontoon bridges and ran across. When the Egyptians tried to follow, they blew up the bridges and killed them all!"

The mother looked down her nose at her son and said, "Is that *really* what she told you?"

Her son put his head down and said, "No. But you wouldn't believe the whopper she tried to get us to swallow!"

Hard to blame the kid, isn't it? Sometimes the stuff God does is a little unbelievable. Bombs and pontoon bridges seem a lot easier to believe than plagues and parting seas. That's why God can't always let us in on what He's up to. There are times we just wouldn't understand. Habakkuk the prophet is complaining to God because things just don't seem right. The bad guys are winning and the good guys are losing. The world seems to be spinning out of control.

"Where are You?" Habakkuk asks. "What are You going to do about all of this?"

God's response? "You wouldn't get it if I explained it to you."

Not a very satisfying answer. But sometimes it's all we get. God works in ways and on timetables that don't seem to make sense to us. When we confront Him about His seeming lack of participation, there is often a deafening silence. He's quiet—not because He's not capable of telling us. He's quiet because we wouldn't understand even if He did. Or if we *could* understand we probably wouldn't believe it.

So if things don't seem fair or right to you today, it's okay to complain to God. He's a big God and quite capable of handling your disappointment with His management system of life. But if He doesn't seem to be quite clear in explaining things to you or He seems not to say anything at all, don't take it personally. Remember Habakkuk and a million others of us who have voiced our complaints as well. He's not being aloof, distant, or uncaring. He simply knows you won't understand. Or worse, if He told you what He was *really* up to, it might scare you to death and send you running for the hills!

Sometimes, out of His great love for you, He just knows you're a lot better off if you don't know. That may not always be comforting, but sometimes it's the best He can do because you wouldn't believe it anyway! That's God's Word for you today.

> **God can't always let us in on what**
> **He's up to because there are times we just**
> **wouldn't understand.**

52

INSIDE-OUT PRAISE

*Even though the fig trees have no blossoms,
and there are no grapes on the vines; even though
the olive crop fails, and the fields lie empty and barren;
even though the flocks die in the fields, and the cattle
barns are empty, yet I will rejoice in the Lord! I will
be joyful in the God of my salvation!*
(Habakkuk 3:17–18)

I met a guy a week and a half ago whom I absolutely fell in love with. His name is Ben, and he is 82. He was raking up rocks in the yard of the pastor I was staying with. He wasn't doing it for pay—he was just doing it to be helpful. He said he remembered me from speaking at his church before, and then with a smile and a wink, he said he had been thinking about staying home this Sunday, but since it was me speaking he would go ahead and come. I laughed and said, "Thanks."

In the course of our conversation Ben talked about how he had started coming to church. It was following a cerebral hemorrhage he had suffered three years before. During his recuperation his wife invited him, and he went. He said he had missed only two Sundays since. He talked with me about his life's journey, explaining how he had suffered a heart attack, a stroke, and cancer in addition to the cerebral hemorrhage. Then, with his broad smile, he described his life as "blessed." I was in absolute awe of this man. When I walked away from him I felt blessed too—just for having met him!

There's something special about people who can praise God regardless of what is going on around them or with them. For most of us our praise is "outside-in." If things are going well around us, we can praise God. If the bills are paid, the kids are obeying, and the traffic is light, we can praise God. If our health is good, we're happy with our jobs, and we got enough sleep, we can praise God. But how about when things *aren't* going our way? Maybe not so much.

Being able to praise God in spite of what's going on around us is very special. That kind of praise is *inside-out.* It's praise that is rooted in commitment. It's praise that comes from the certainty of God's ultimate provision. It's praise that is dripping with faith. Praising God the way Habakkuk talks about takes a heart that is anchored in God. It flows out of joy, not just being happy. It flows out of peace, not out of being in control. It flows out of devotion, not just having everything going our way.

Habakkuk had that kind of praise. So did my new friend Ben. Do you? That's God's Word for you today.

Praising God in spite of what's going on around us is very special. That kind of praise is **inside-out.**

53

YOU MAKE GOD SING

The Lord your God is living among you.
He is a mighty savior. He will take delight in you
with gladness. With his love, he will calm all your fears.
He will rejoice over you with joyful songs.
(Zephaniah 3:17)

Have you ever had anyone in your life who makes you just want to sing? Maybe it's that child or grandchild you hold in your arms—so warm, innocent, pure, giving you such joy that you can hardly breathe. When they're lying there quiet or asleep, do you find yourself humming? Maybe it's a song you know or just a tune flowing out of your heart. All you know is that you want this moment to last forever. You want them always to stay small and remain in the safety of your arms. You want this child to feel the love you have for them because you know you will never find the words. You would give your life for this child. You look forward to giving your life *to* them.

That's how God is with you. You bring Him more joy than you can imagine. Zephaniah says that God has that same instinct to sing over you as you do with your kids. Have you ever wondered what kind of songs God sings? Maybe He sings songs of Joy—laughing at all those funny things you do that tickle His Divine Heart. Maybe He sings songs of Comfort because He saw how scared you were today. Maybe He sings songs of Hope because He knows that's what you need as you face the week ahead. Or maybe He sings songs of Love—because everything about you makes Him so glad He made you!

Today the God of heaven, who is Mighty, Powerful and Good, delights in you. He's singing over you out of joy. Oh, I know—you don't feel all that lovable and enjoyable. You've thrown tantrums, spilled stuff, and made a mess of things. And yes, you haven't always followed what you've been told. But you're still His Child. And when you're finally quiet and still and let Him close, He just can't help Himself. In spite of all of your shortcomings, you are still pure and innocent to Him, and you bring Him so much joy He can hardly breathe.

So don't be surprised if sometime in a moment of spiritual connection you hear a faint, hushed melody you don't quite recognize. It's just a grateful Father enjoying a special moment with His child. It's just God—singing over you again. That's God's Word for you today.

Today the God of heaven, who is
Mighty, Powerful, and Good, delights in you.
He's singing over you out of joy!

54

THE GLORY DAYS

"The glory of this present house will be greater than the
glory of the former house," says the Lord Almighty.
(Haggai 2:9 NIV)

Thirty years ago I worked with a couple whose marriage had fallen apart. As with most couples, there were issues. But theirs had gone underground until there was a complete breakdown. He left, filed for divorce, and never looked back. But then a miracle happened. On the day the divorce was to be final, God broke his heart. He came home, asked his wife for forgiveness, and they began to rebuild. It was shaky at first, but then after a few more breakthroughs, they got over "the hump" and on their way.

What's interesting is that for all they had been through, their new relationship was much better than their old one. In fact, it was even better than when the old one was at its best! It was as though God took the remnants of their past relationship, forged it in the fire, and made it stronger, more durable, *better*. Now, thirty years later, they are happier than ever and still going strong.

God is not just a wonderful Creator—He is also an amazing Rebuilder! His promise through Haggai is that He would take the remnants of what was left of His temple and make it more glorious and beautiful than ever. If people thought the "glory days" of the temple were the days of old, they were mistaken. Those were good days, for sure. But the true "glory days" were those that were yet to come. When it was built it was beautiful. When it was rebuilt it would be *better*!

God can do that for you too. He created you. He can also rebuild you. Sometimes you may look at your life and feel there's just not much there to work with. But for God it's more than enough. Some days you may hope that you can just get back to the way things were. But it probably won't happen. As the old adage says, "You can't step in the same stream twice." Too much water has passed by. But the good news is—it can be *better*. Your life can be better. Your job can be better. Your relationships can be better. What may seem hopeless or helpless to you in this moment right now can be made into something wonderful by the Master Craftsman.

Don't wish for the past. Look to the future! Give to God the tattered remains of the remnants of whatever needs to be mended, and just watch what He can do. For Him the glory days are never the days that are behind us. They are the days that are yet to come! That's God's Word for you today.

God is not just a wonderful Creator—
He is also an amazing Rebuilder!

55

LEADING AND INTERCEDING

> *"Tell him, 'This is what the Lord of*
> *heaven's Armies says: Here is the man called the*
> *Branch. He will branch out from where he is and*
> *build the Temple of the Lord. Yes, he will build the*
> *Temple of the Lord. Then he will receive royal honor*
> *and will rule as king from his throne. He will also*
> *serve as priest from his throne, and there will be*
> *perfect harmony between his two roles.'"*
> **(Zechariah 6:12–13)**

You gotta love how God sets up the coming of His Son into the world. The two verses above are written about Joshua, who is the son of the high priest, Jehozadak. Joshua is going to be anointed as king, even though he is a priest. It's unheard of. But the name *Joshua* is actually the Hebrew name for *Jesus.*

So this passage is also a beautiful prophecy about the coming Messiah! Jesus would be both the King of Kings and the final High Priest. His calling would be to both lead and intercede. He would be given power to rule. He would also be given the responsibility to redeem. He would sit on a throne. He would also hang on a cross. He would overturn the tables of moneychangers in the temple who were ripping off the people. He would also hold children in His arms and bless them. Leading and interceding—it's a hard mix of roles, but one both Joshua and Jesus would have to navigate with courage and wisdom.

How do *you* do with those two roles? As those who wear His name, we too are called to both lead and intercede. Do you act "kingly"? Do you stand up for those who are being unjustly accused or oppressed? Do you use the power God has given you to do good whenever and wherever you can? Do you lead by making hard decisions when hard decisions have to be made? Do you confront those who need to be confronted? Do you stand for goodness, even when those around you are trying to bend you toward evil?

Are you also "priestly"? Do you live with a kind and gentle spirit that is soothing to those you have contact with? Do you calm troubled hearts and help extinguish the flames of anger in the lives of those around you? Do you act with grace, mercy, and patience toward those who are wounded, struggling, and weary? Are you a healer? Are you a helper? Are you a giver of hope? The balance of power and grace has always been a sacred dance, one Jesus modeled for us very well.

My experience has been that most of us demonstrate more of one side of Christ than the other. Most who are powerful find it difficult to be merciful. Many who are kind find it hard to act with firmness when it's needed. Christ is the perfect mixture of both. He is All Powerful and He is All Merciful. He is King and He is Priest. He showed us how to lead and He showed us how to intercede.

The world is still in need of that wonderful image of God. Be strong today. But let that strength be wrapped in gentleness. Be a king. Be a priest. Be the living example of Christ whom this world is looking for. Go lead and intercede! That's God's Word for you today.

Christ is the perfect mixture of power and mercy.

56

THE HEALER IS HERE!

For you who fear my name, the Sun of Righteousness
will rise with healing in his wings.
(Malachi 4:2)

A Healer—is there any greater need in this world of ours than for that? Everywhere you look you see hurt, pain, and brokenness. And you don't have to look far. All across our communities we see the opioid crisis and the epidemic of addiction. Just around the corner are abuse, neglect, and domestic violence. Right next door is the troubled teen, the shaky marriage, the lonely widow. Who are we kidding? The hurt is right here. It's in our own homes, in our own families, and sitting in this chair. If there were ever a time when a Healer would be most welcomed, it would be now. Thank God—He is here!

This prophetic passage about Jesus was one of the last written before His coming. It would be another four hundred years until Jesus walked among us, but the hurting would be waiting on Him when He got here. And He would bring His healing to all He met. This "Sun of Righteousness" Malachi wrote about would be the living, breathing "Jehovah Rapha," "the God who heals us." Blind eyes would see. Lame legs would walk. Deaf ears would hear. Broken hearts would be mended. Guilty consciences would be cleansed. Darkened souls would be made new. Dead people would live again. Jesus would soar into this limping, bleeding world with healing in His wings. Whoever He touched was made whole. No wonder the Jews longed so much for that coming Messiah! The Great Physician became flesh. Let the healing begin!

Do *you* long for Him as well? I'm guessing there are more than a few of us who could use the touch of the wing of our Healer. Jesus, who was prophesied about by Malachi and witnessed by those in the first century, walks among us still. He is *our* Jehovah Rapha. He can still heal bodies, touch hearts, save souls, and fix homes.

And He can touch you—whoever you are and however you need to be healed. Reach out to Him today. Lay your pain before Him as He passes by you right where you are.

Give Him your broken heart. Give Him your weary spirit. Give Him your hurting body. Invite the Sun of Righteousness to rise with healing in His Wings for you today.

Maybe Malachi's words weren't meant for just the waiting Jews. Maybe they were written for all of us throughout history who are in dire need of a Healer. Maybe, just maybe, they were written for *you*! That's God's Word for you today.

***Jesus soared into this limping,
bleeding world with healing in His wings!***

57

DIVINE INTERRUPTIONS

MATTHEW 1:18–25

This is how Jesus the Messiah was born.
His mother, Mary, was engaged to be married to
Joseph. But before the marriage took place, while
she was still a virgin, she became pregnant through
the power of the Holy Spirit.
(Matthew 1:18)

Has God ever wrecked your plans? He does that sometimes. You're just cruising right along with your life with everything under control, just the way it's supposed to be, and—*bam!* Here comes God with one of His divine interruptions. It wasn't on your radar screen. It wasn't in your plans. It may not be a direction in which you would ever think to go or a choice you would ever make on your own. But God puts it in your lap and in your life and now everything's changed. Has that ever happened to you?

It happened to Mary and Joseph. They were engaged to get married and had their whole lives planned out. Then, out of nowhere, God sends an angel to them and totally wrecks their lives. Mary's pregnant with the Son of God. How's she going to explain *that* to her family? Joseph plans to quietly break things off and God sends an angel to him and tells him to stay. Can you imagine the ribbing he was going to get from the other guys? And the kicker? Their son is going to be the Messiah! That was nowhere on their radar screen!

Ultimately it would be a marvelous thing, a wonderful thing! It would be the *most sacred* responsibility any couple had ever been given. Jesus would save the world! But first He would totally undo this young couple's lives. The story of Joseph and Mary reminds us that sometimes to get to "marvelous" you have to put up with "messy"!

You may need to remind yourself of that today. Because sooner or later, *you* are going to encounter a divine interruption. Oh, probably not a virgin birth interruption—I think we're done with those. But I'll bet you that somewhere along the nice, smooth path you've planned, God is going to wreck you a bit. It may be a job change—and one you don't think is exactly the best career opportunity. It may be becoming a foster parent or a guardian to a child—when you were done with parenting. It may be a change of positions, a change of communities, or a change of ministries. You may hate it, resent it, and even be angry at first. But stay with it. God doesn't interrupt our lives without purpose. He doesn't get joy out of our chaos.

But sometimes His purposes are important enough to inconvenience His children whom He loves. Sometimes there is a world to save. Other times it may be simply a child who needs to be saved. But if God redirects you, trust me—there's a need to meet that's at the other end of your discomfort. As big a pill that this may be for you to swallow, your personal comfort isn't the highest thing on God's list. Changing the world is.

One day you'll look back and see what a marvelous thing God did. But until you get to "marvelous," you might want to prepare yourself for a good bit of "messy"! That's God's Word for you today.

Your personal comfort isn't the highest thing on God's list. Changing the world is.

58

HIGHS AND LOWS

MATTHEW 4:1–11

*Then Jesus was led by the Spirit into the
wilderness to be tempted there by the devil.*
(Matthew 4:1)

I woke up today with a headache. That's not unusual for
most pastors on a Monday. The headache wasn't a result
of anything bad—it was actually the result of something
good. I had enjoyed a busy weekend with lots of activity and
excitement, meeting several new people at church, engaging
in several stimulating conversations, and topping it off with a
few hours of great food and fellowship with our folks.

But all the spent adrenaline on Sunday left my body going
through withdrawal today. It's the low that often comes after
a high. Yesterday I felt as if I could go forever. Today I felt

as if I were plowing through mud. Yesterday I could take on the world. Today you could knock me over with a feather. At the close of yesterday's service it felt as if God were right here. Today it felt as if He were nowhere around. Highs and lows—they're a part of the journey. Maybe it's something you can relate to. Jesus certainly could.

Don't you find it interesting that Jesus goes immediately from the exhilarating thrill of His baptism, when the Holy Spirit descends on Him like a dove, to a forty-day face-to-face with the devil in the wilderness? He goes from the affirming voice of His Father to being hungry, tired, and repeatedly tempted. From the cheers of heaven to the jeers of hell, from the highest highs to the lowest lows. I think it's the nature of life.

I also think it's the strategy of the evil one. He likes taking the wind out of our sails. He likes trying to steal the joy out of our journey. He loves it when he can catch us at a moment when we're spent. He's like a boxer waiting for us to drop our guard, and then *boom!* We're on the mat trying to figure out how we got there. We're also looking for the strength to get up.

Jesus did something we can all learn from: He leaned in to what He *knew,* not how He *felt.* Feelings are powerful, but they're often not truth. Jesus reminded Himself of who He *was,* not who the devil tried to convince Him He was. He also held onto the Word. Satan quoted scripture to Jesus. Jesus quoted it right back to him. He held on long enough for Satan to leave. Then God lifted Him up again.

So if you're on a "high" right now, enjoy every minute of it. Highs are wonderful moments and should be thoroughly embraced. But just know there's a "low" right around the corner. When it comes, don't panic. And don't let the enemy overcome you or push you into a cave of depression, fear, or despair. Lean in to what you *know*. God is with you always. These feelings will pass. Remember who you *are:* a child of the living God! And lean into God's Word. Claim the promises of Scripture over and over until you reach the other side of your wilderness.

God's Word will be your Life Raft when these rough waters come. Highs and lows are a part of the journey. But don't worry. Just like Jesus, your Father will be with you in both. That's God's Word for you today.

Feelings are powerful, but they're often not truth.

59

THE MAN WHO AMAZED JESUS

*But the officer said, "Lord, I am not worthy
to have you come into my home. Just say the word from
where you are, and my servant will be healed."...
When Jesus heard this, he was amazed. Turning to
those who were following him, he said, "I tell you the
truth, I haven't seen faith like this in all Israel!"*
(Matthew 8:8, 10)

This story ought to give us all great hope in our journey with God. I don't know about you, but I often feel too unworthy to ask God for big stuff. Maybe I'm afraid I just won't ask Him the right way. But then I read about this guy. He humbly but boldly came to Jesus with a request for Him to heal his servant. He had no "inside tracks" with God.

He wasn't a priest, a disciple, or even a Jew. He was a Roman military officer. Because the Romans ruled over the Jews and many Romans took advantage of Jews and oppressed them, they were regarded as "the enemy." In fact, the Jews were counting on the Messiah (Jesus) to overthrow the Romans!

But in spite of the fact that he had no religious connection, most likely knew next to nothing about the Torah, the Psalms, or even who Jesus really was, he believed. He *so* believed that he didn't even think Jesus had to come to his home and touch his servant to heal him. "Just say the word," the man said, "and he'll be healed." He *amazed* Jesus. Now that's something most of us don't do every day!

Jesus was moved by this simple faith. He's not impressed by church positions or religious heritage. He's not influenced by Bible knowledge or doctrinal correctness. Jesus was moved because the man believed in *Him*. While the Jews were arguing over whether Jesus could heal on the Sabbath or eat without washing and other such nonsense, along came a Roman soldier who simply *believed*. We don't know his background or how he came to hear about Jesus and what He could do. But he *believed*. He didn't think Jesus had to pray the right prayer or perform any religious rite or even come to his house. Surrounded by people who were all trying to prove how important they were to Jesus, this Roman officer came humbly and aware of his unworthiness. How refreshing this man must have been for Jesus! Jesus was amazed by him.

How about you? When's the last time you amazed Jesus? When's the last time you came in faith and really believed Jesus would hear and honor your request? You don't have to have it all together. You don't have to have deep theological roots. You don't have to understand all the mysteries of the Trinity, the Incarnation, or divine healing. You just have to believe in Jesus and what He can do.

The religious folks may have not cared too much for the Roman officer. They may have thought he was a no-good pagan. But Jesus had another name for him: Amazing. Now that's a name I'd love Jesus to call me! That's God's Word for you today.

When's the last time you amazed _Jesus?_

60

JESUS IS WILLING

*A man with leprosy came and knelt in front
of Jesus, begging to be healed. "If you are willing,
you can heal me and make me clean," he said. Moved
with compassion, Jesus reached out and touched him.
"I am willing," he said. "Be healed!"*
(Mark 1:40–41)

Jesus is willing. In a world full of reluctant people, He is willing. When you find yourself surrounded by so many who don't want to get involved, Jesus is willing. When it feels as if no one cares, no one has time, and no one is interested, He is willing. Even when you look around and find all your friends and all those you had counted on are gone, Jesus is willing.

Jesus is willing to listen to you. That's rare. Just look around. Everyone is so busy. Everyone is in a hurry. Everyone has their own problems, issues, and life filled to overflowing. Just look at them: heads down, eyes glued to the screens of their phones, checking their email, checking their messages, checking their calendars. Who has time for you? Who has time to listen to your hurts, your concerns, your pressures, your fears?

Jesus does. Surrounded by a huge crowd of people, Jesus stops for one leper. We don't even know his name. But Jesus did. He knew who he was and what he needed. And He had time to listen.

Jesus is willing to help you. Lepers were thought to be beyond help. They were put in colonies out away from the community where they could stay to themselves. No one even wanted to be near them, much less help them. But Jesus specialized in being there for those who needed Him most. What do you need today? Where do you need a lift, a boost, or a helping hand? What could Jesus give you that would bless you beyond words today? Then seek Him. He is willing.

Jesus is willing to touch you. This little part of the story is the most startling. *Nobody* touched lepers. They didn't even get within several feet of them. They were diseased. They were disgusting. They were unclean. They had disfigured bodies and decaying limbs, and they smelled.

Jesus could have just spoken the word and the man would have been healed. He had healed others from a distance—why not this man? Because this man *needed* to be touched. He needed to feel the hand of human kindness that he had not felt in a long, long time. To be touched was to be *accepted*—just as he was. My guess is that simply feeling the touch of Jesus was almost as meaningful as feeling the leprosy leave his body. Jesus wasn't just healing him—He was *welcoming* him, welcoming him back, welcoming him *home.*

What do *you* need from Jesus today? Do you feel alienated, forgotten, or abandoned? Do you feel that no one has any time, energy, or interest left for you? Are you in need of healing, a touch, or the welcoming embrace of coming home?

Kneel for a moment in front of Jesus. He'll meet you right where you are. He is not a reluctant God. He is willing. That's God Word for you today.

What could Jesus give you that would bless you beyond words today? He is willing!

61

WITH *BEFORE* FOR!

MARK 3:13–19

He appointed twelve that they might be
with him and that he might send them out to preach
and to have authority to drive out demons.
(Mark 3:14–15 NIV)

Today's passage marks a momentous event. It was the ordaining of the Twelve. This would be the group that would go out and rock the world. They would be the group Jesus would leave in charge of establishing His church on earth. They would preach as He preached. They would heal as He healed. They would cast out demons as He cast out demons. Their names would be forever immortalized in Christianity. But they had to do one very important thing first: they had to be *with* Him.

This little phrase is so subtle that we almost miss it. But we can't. It was the key to their success. Before they were to work *for* Jesus they had to spend time *with* Jesus. So for three years they followed Him. They listened. They learned. They asked dumb questions. Jesus gave them answers that left them scratching their heads. They stepped out on water. They sank like a rock. They marveled at His miracles. They were shamed by His compassion. They learned that greatness was serving and that people who push their way to the front get put at the back.

He taught them to pray. He taught them to forgive. He taught them how to live like men of God. He showed them how to die. He proved to them that God was greater even than the grave. After spending that kind of time with Jesus, they were now ready to take on the world for Jesus!

The same is true for us. Do you really want to do something amazing for Jesus? Do you want to be a force for God where you work, where you live, or where you go to school? Do you want God to empower you as a teacher, a leader, or a worker in His kingdom? Do you want to live a life that will truly be memorable? Do you want to leave a legacy one day? The key is probably not in working harder or longer. The key may be in what you do before you actually do anything.

Be with Jesus. Spend some meaningful time with your Model and Mentor. Listen to His words. Learn from His life. Ask Him your questions and heed His advice. Let Him breathe both correction and encouragement into you. Let Him show you how to live, how to serve, how to die. Be *with* Jesus—each day, every day, because it's being *with* Him that prepares you to live *for* Him. That's God's Word for you today.

Be *with Jesus before you work* for *Jesus!*

62

DON'T GO IT ALONE

They went to the olive grove called Gethsemane,
and Jesus said, "Sit here while I go and pray."
He took Peter, James, and John with him, and he
became deeply troubled and distressed. He told them,
"My soul is crushed with grief to the point of death.
Stay here and keep watch with me."
(Mark 14:32–34)

I got a call today from a guy in the community who doesn't attend our church. He was looking for some advice on dealing with an issue he's been struggling with. He's a strong guy, a fitness trainer by trade. But he was facing something he didn't know what to do with. So he called our church at random and happened to end up with me. As he shared his struggle and confessed his need for help, I could tell it wasn't easy for him. I gave him some counsel, informed him about some available resources, and told him that I believed he could overcome with God's help.

Then I gave him one more piece of advice: "Don't go at this alone," I said. "You've taken the hardest step of admitting your struggle—now take the next hardest step. Find a few godly men to share your journey. You weren't made to do this alone." Then we prayed together.

Jesus models this for us. As He faces His darkest hours leading up the cross, He retreats to the Garden of Gethsemane to pray. Though He leaves most of the Twelve in the outer area, He takes His three closest friends into the inner place with Him. *"My soul is crushed with grief to the point of death. Stay here and keep watch with me."* The King of Kings, God in the flesh, the Alpha and Omega asks for the support of a few close friends.

I'd say that if Jesus found the support and company of a few godly friends helpful in His time of struggle, *we* might want to consider that too! It's not a sign of weakness—it's a sign of humility and wisdom. We were *designed* to live in community and to share the journey with others. To try to do life alone is foolish and prideful.

So what are you facing these days? Are you going it alone? Are you sure you should? God gave you others to multiply your joy and divide your sorrows. You need their support. You need their encouragement. You need their counsel. You need their accountability. You need their prayers. Hopefully you're not facing a Gethsemane kind of experience this week. But when you do, do what Jesus did: take a friend or two with you.

Just as God told Adam in the garden, "It's not good for man to be alone." It's still not. That's God's Word for you today.

If Jesus needed the support of a few godly friends, we might want to consider that too!

63

HE WAS THINKING OF YOU

*At noon, darkness fell across the whole land
until three o'clock. Then at three o'clock Jesus
called out with a loud voice, Eloi, Eloi, lema
sabachthani? which means "My God, my God,
why have you abandoned me?"*
(Mark 15:33–34)

There's a mystery surrounding Christ on the cross.
I don't think we can honestly wrap our minds
around it. He was fully God, yet He was fully man. In His
human form He obviously suffered pain as all of us do. He
also experienced death. But our verses today highlight a piece
that leaves us scratching our heads. If He was God Himself,
how could He be *abandoned* by God? Some theologians say

He was somehow mysteriously separated from the Trinity in that moment, that He didn't just take on our sins but also "became" sin and thus couldn't be a part of God. Others think He maintained His deity but let Himself feel the fullness of the human horror of dying that horrible death so He might fully identify with the depths of our human struggle. As I said before, I personally think it's a beautiful, powerful, incredible mystery, the fullness of which I don't think we can totally comprehend.

One thing I would throw into the mix, though—I think Jesus was leaning upon His knowledge of Scripture for the strength to endure this moment. Feeling "abandoned" by God would certainly be understandable for anyone experiencing what He was going through. But His words are also the first verse of Psalm 22, which would be words He would know. I think He was quoting this psalm because it reminded Him of His purpose and the impact of this moment. Jesus was heard quoting the first verse of Psalm 22, but listen to the last two verses: *Future generations will hear about the wonders of the Lord. His righteous acts will be told to those not yet born. They will hear about everything he has done* (Psalm 22:30–31). He knew that His horror would be our Hope.

Are you sitting down? When Jesus was dying on the cross, I believe He was thinking of *you.* You are that "future generation." You are that one of those "not yet born." Jesus leaned on the Word of God in that horrible moment and reminded Himself that He was doing this for *you*!

So as you reflect on Jesus's words, let the mystery of the cross speak to you. Let it remind you that Jesus identifies with your deepest, darkest moments of pain and suffering. He even knows what it means to feel abandoned by God. But let them also remind you of why it's so important to bury the Word of God in your heart. You never know when you might need God's Word to give you strength. And never forget this: You are *always* on the mind of Jesus! You were the reason He came. You were on His mind as He lived and loved and healed. You were on His mind in His last dying breaths. You are *still* on His mind as He stands by the Father smiling upon you today.

After all these years of ministry, I have to confess that the cross is still a mystery to me. But one thing I'm sure of: it had a lot to do with *you*! That's God's Word for you today.

> **When Jesus was dying on the cross,**
> **He was thinking of you.**

64

YOU'RE CLOSER THAN YOU THINK!

When he had finished speaking,
he said to Simon, "Now go out where it is
deeper, and let down your nets to catch some fish."
"Master," Simon replied, "we worked hard all last
night and didn't catch a thing. But if you say so, I'll let the
nets down again." And this time their nets were so
full of fish they began to tear! A shout for help brought
their partners in the other boat, and soon both boats
were filled with fish and on the verge of sinking.
(Luke 5:4–7)

Some years ago I was coaching a church planter who was having a hard time getting his new church going. He talked about his growing frustration and was ready to quit. His funding was running out, his workers were getting tired, and even his key leaders, who believed in his vision, were becoming burned out by feeling that they were running as hard as they could but getting no traction. People just weren't coming. We spent some time that week praying and looking at options.

One thing we noticed was that there seemed to an "invisible barrier" that people wouldn't cross. Because of their routine traffic patterns, people would drive across the freeway one way but not the other. We explored some options for moving his meeting location. God opened a door for a movie theater that had previously not been available. The church was moved just a few miles—and it flourished! Had the church planter quit, a thriving and impactful congregation would never have come to be. Sometimes success is a lot closer than you think. It's just a little farther out than where you are.

Most of us could identify with Peter's reaction to Jesus in our scripture today. We've all been there. We've worked really hard to plant a church, get a ministry going, make a difference, or help someone we love find a better path. After a while the fatigue sets in. We're out of ideas, out of energy, and out of strength. Then we feel God nudge us to go again. "Go out a little deeper." "Try this instead of that." "Ask them to come to church with you one more time." "Don't quit."

Like Peter, we argue with God that we've done all we know to do. But God knows something we don't know—He knows that the heart of that person we think is never going to change is becoming open. He knows that you're about to have a breakthrough in that class you teach or that ministry you lead. He knows that out *there,* just a little deeper than where you are now, is where the fish are. You're closer to success than you think—if you just don't quit.

I don't know where you are on your journey today, but I'm guessing that you might be among those who have thought of giving up at one point. You're tired. You're frustrated. You're out of ideas. I totally get that. Many pastors feel that way every Monday.

But don't quit. Before you throw in the towel, take a moment to listen to what Jesus may be saying. Maybe you're just an idea away, a week away, another attempt away, or a prayer away from making a breakthrough. Maybe out there, just a little deeper, God is waiting for you with more than you can imagine.

Throw the net out one more time—and get ready for the haul of your life! That's God's Word for today.

> *Maybe out there, just a little deeper,*
> *God is waiting for you with more*
> *than you can imagine.*

65

LIVING OUT OF THE OVERFLOW

*Despite Jesus' instructions, the report
of his power spread even faster, and vast crowds came to
hear him preach and to be healed of their diseases. But
Jesus often withdrew to the wilderness for prayer.*
(Luke 5:15–16)

"Live out of the overflow." Have you ever heard that
before? It's really a good statement. In fact, it ought
to be our motto for life. It means that we should make sure
we are filling ourselves up enough to be able to give ourselves
away to others.

Many of us aren't very good at that. Oh, we give ourselves
away *a lot.* We teach, we advise, we encourage, we serve,
we solve problems, and we help a lot of people fix a lot of

different situations they find themselves in. We take care of our families. We take care of our parents. We take care of our friends.

But for many of us, the one person we *don't* take care of is ourselves. Do that long enough and you won't be taking care of anybody!

I remember reading our scripture today at a time when I was running really hard in ministry. I was addicted to the adrenaline and stuck in a pace that wasn't sustainable. I read this passage and it seemed to jump off the page at me: "Jesus often withdrew to the wilderness for prayer."

Then it hit me. Even the Son of God didn't do ministry 24/7. He needed a break from the people, the demands, the hordes of people calling His name. He needed to recharge. He needed to refresh His Spirit. He needed time with His Father. He needed to empty His heart of His pain and to fill His soul with the breath of God. So I wrote in the margin of my Bible that day, "If Jesus needed to do this, so do I!"

So stop. Stop the "running until you can't run anymore." Stop the "doing until you can't do anymore." Stop the "going until you can't go anymore." I know you think you can't take time for yourself, but you can. Sometimes those who are needy, hurting, and suffering just need to wait. Jesus walked away from the crowds when there was still much ministry that needed to be done. My guess is there were many who thought He was being selfish, uncaring, and unkind. But He was actually doing exactly what He needed to do, for *them* and for Him! He was living out of the overflow. He was filling Himself up so that He would be more able to pour Himself out.

There was a living spring within Him, just as there is within us. But the pump of that spring needs to be primed from time to time. If not, then the living water stops flowing. That's when we *all* lose.

I'm not asking you to quit everything you're doing, though my guess is there are probably a few things you should let go of. What I *am* saying is that you need to set a pace for your life of pouring in as well as giving out. Don't wait until you *have* to take a break to take one. Don't wait until you're as dry as dust or wiped out with fatigue before you let yourself breathe.

Do what Jesus did: walk away. Give yourself some regular time to get with the Father and renew your spirit. Read, listen, sing, rest, or sit at someone else's feet and take it in. Prime the pump of that living stream within you. Let yourself be poured into until it gushes out of you. That's living out of the overflow. That's what Jesus did. Maybe you should too. That's God's Word for you today.

Don't wait until you're as dry as dust or wiped out with fatigue before you let yourself breathe.

66

WE'RE TEAMMATES, NOT ENEMIES

John said to Jesus, "Master, we saw someone using your name to cast out demons, but we told him to stop because he isn't in our group." But Jesus said, "Don't stop him! Anyone who is not against you is for you."
(Luke 9:49–50)

I was talking recently to a college freshman who had grown up in our church. He's attending a local Christian university. In his religion class the professor told them that their particular tribe in the Christian faith is the only "true church," that they will be the only ones in heaven.

Let that sink in for a moment. He wasn't saying that Christ followers alone will be there but that their *special brand* of Christ followers would be the only ones there! All others aren't just "wrong" in their theology—they're "out." I found it more than a little bold. I thought it was a bit offensive—mainly, I guess, because I'm one of the ones who supposedly aren't going to get in!

The disciples wanted to stop a guy who was invoking Jesus's name to do some good. The guy wasn't a part of their "tribe." Maybe they were jealous because he was doing some things they couldn't do. Perhaps he was drawing a little crowd of his own and they felt he shouldn't be doing that. Maybe he didn't dress the way they thought he should dress, talk the way they thought he should talk, or act the way they thought he should act. Or maybe they just felt that their group should be the only ones allowed to do such stuff because, after all, they were "the disciples."

Whatever their reasoning was, Jesus disagreed with them. His response was "Don't stop him. Anyone who is not against you is for you." In other words, "Get over yourselves. I alone determine who can use My name, not you. Embrace him as a teammate, not an enemy!"

That's a good word for us. In a deeply divided world Christ followers should demonstrate *unity*. It's okay to have different opinions about theology and practices. It's okay to sing different kinds of songs in different ways. It's okay to perform different kinds of rituals in different manners. Some of us baptize by sprinkling water on people. Some of us do it by pouring water over their heads. My particular tribe baptizes by dunking people completely under water.

But guess what—Jesus alone is the one who forgives sin. It's His name that we minister and it's His work we are doing. And these people we are serving? They are His people, not ours. So before we take a shot at someone else who is doing this Jesus thing a little different from us, let's remember again the words of Jesus: "Anyone who is not against you is for you."

We're not enemies, folks—we're teammates. Let's act like it. That's God's Word for you today.

In a deeply divided world Christ followers should demonstrate **unity.**

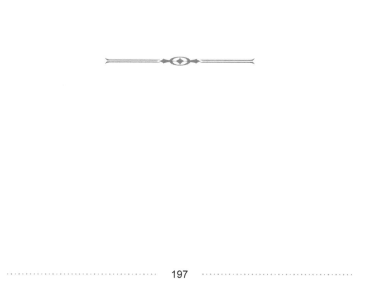

67

WELCOME HOME

LUKE 15:11–24

So he returned home to his father. And while
he was still a long way off, his father saw him coming.
Filled with love and compassion, he ran to his son,
embraced him, and kissed him.
(Luke 15:20)

I read a story recently of an eleven-year-old boy in Miami who ran away from home. He was upset because he didn't want to go to camp, but his mother was making him go anyway. So he took off. When they discovered that he was missing, his family panicked. The world is not a safe place and they were fearful something bad would happen to him. They called the police and the search was on.

The word soon began to spread, and neighbors and other family members joined in the search. They looked for him in places he might go and called other families whom he might run to. They called his friends who might know where he was. No one had seen him or knew where he was.

A local television station picked up the story and began coverage. They sent out one of their helicopters to show footage of the people scouring the area and to do interviews with the family. Suddenly the reporter in the helicopter spotted him. He wasn't hurt or kidnapped or even lost—he was on the roof of his own home, taking a nap while hiding. I'm sure there was a part of that mother that wanted to strangle him, but she didn't. She hugged him relentlessly. As much of a problem as he had caused, he was *home* safe and sound.

Jesus says that's how God is with us. Sometimes we get lost. Sometimes it's intentional. We just want to try to do life on our own. Sometimes it's accidental. We can begin wandering a bit and not realize how far from the Father we're going. Sometimes we get lost because we're hiding. We're hiding from our past. We're hiding from our future. We're hiding from pain, fear, or someone or something that has hurt us.

Then something happens, and we decide we want to go back. We're often so overwhelmed by the shame of our stupidity that we can hardly bear it. How will we be received? Can God really forgive us after all we've done?

Jesus describes God's reaction to His lost children in this story so there would be no mistake about God's response. God *runs* to us! It doesn't matter to Him why we left. It doesn't matter where we went. It doesn't matter what we did. What *does* matter is that we're *back*. We're *home*!

Are you hiding? Have you wandered away? Do you find yourself a bit farther from God today than you know you ought to be? Come down from whatever roof you're hiding on. Come back from whatever place you've wandered to. Let go of the shame. Let go of the guilt. Let go of the fear and the pain. Take a step in the direction of Your Father and He will *run* to meet you with joy and compassion. He'll embrace you with His love and kiss you with His grace.

And what will He say to you? That one's easy. "Welcome *home*!" That's God's Word for you today.

Take a step in the direction of your Father and He will* run *to meet you with joy and compassion.

68

HE BECAME ONE OF US

The Word became human and made
his home among us. He was full of unfailing
love and faithfulness. And we have seen his glory,
the glory of the Father's one and only Son.
(John 1:14)

There's a great old story of a grandfather who came over to see his daughter and young toddler grandson. The grandson had been quite a handful that day, so the mother put him in a playpen as punishment. When the grandfather walked in, the young boy squealed with delight, stood, and held out his arms for his grandfather to pick him up. But when the grandfather started to reach down for him, his daughter intervened. "No," she said sternly. "He's not been obedient today. He has to stay in the playpen a while longer."

The grandfather looked sadly at the boy, who was still standing there with arms outstretched and whimpering. He knew he couldn't undermine his daughter's authority, but his heart was breaking for the child. Then, with a smile, the grandfather knew what he had to do: he stepped over the side and sat down in the playpen with his grandson.

Our passage today is one of the most significant statements, maybe even *the* most significant statement in all of history. God steps down from heaven and becomes a man. The unknowable has made Himself known. The unreachable is now an arm's distance away. The one who was so holy that His Name could not even be spoken takes on a human one. They called Him "Jesus." God, who has forever been shrouded in mystery, can now be seen.

All those things we wanted to know about God have become documented history. We now know how God would speak, how God would act, and what God would do if He were among us. We couldn't leave the confines of our planet, so the Creator stepped into the playpen of earth to be with us. And that changed *everything*.

Now when we want to know how to act, we have a model. Jesus didn't just *tell* us how to live—He *showed* us! He showed us how to treat those we love, those we are uncomfortable around, and even those we hate. He showed us how to deal with those who treat us unfairly and how to be gentle with those who are weaker. He showed us how to love, how to live, and how to give our lives away. God has stepped into our world, into our lives, and into our mess.

So look to Him. Everything you ever wanted to know about God you can find by exploring the life of Jesus. He has become your map, your model, and your measurement. You don't have to wonder any more about what God is like or what He wants from you. God has stepped into your playpen. Follow Jesus. He'll show you the way. That's God's Word for you today.

Jesus is your map, your model,
and your measurement!

69

NOT JUST RELIGIOUS—BUT BORN AGAIN!

JOHN 3:1–17

> *Jesus replied, "I tell you the truth, unless you are born*
> *again, you cannot see the Kingdom of God."*
> **(John 3:3)**

Religious people really struggled with Jesus. They just didn't get it. They thought being right with God was all about following the rules. They believed that the more rules they followed the more holy they were. But they weren't holy. And they weren't happy. For the most part, they were the most angry and frustrated group on the planet.

They still are. Oh, I'm not saying you can't be holy *and* religious. I'm just saying that religious by itself doesn't cut it. That was Nicodemus' story. He was more than just religious. He was a religious *leader*. He set the bar for the rules-followers.

But there was something missing. When He heard Jesus teach, he knew there was something that Jesus had that he didn't. He couldn't deny Jesus's power, but it was more than that. There was something about Jesus that left him wanting more. So he went to Jesus privately to ask Him what it was. And Jesus told him. "You have to start over. You must be born again or you'll never get it."

The phrase "born again" can be and probably should be translated "born from above." Jesus was telling him that he had to be born from above. God wants to be a Father to you and have His Spirit flowing through you. You're not a child of God because you obey all the family rules. You're a child of God because His blood runs through your veins!

Start over, Nicodemus. Become like a child who knows nothing instead of the guy who thinks he knows everything. Just ask the Father to love you into His family. Open your heart to that love and ask His Spirit to live in you and through you. Be born again, Nicky. Be born from above. Then the kingdom of God is all yours.

What a great reminder for all of us! God isn't after religious fanatics. He wants children. Sure, He wants us to pay attention to the family rules, because they're there for a reason. They are there to protect us, provide for us, and help us connect to Him. But the rules don't *change* us. And God desperately wants to change us. He doesn't want rules-followers who are always looking for the "loopholes" to justify what they do. He wants children after His own heart who are seeking to become like Him. He's not interested in people who read their Bibles, say their prayers, and attend church services but then go around angry, frustrated, and resentful. He wants people whose lives overflow with love, joy, peace, patience, kindness, goodness, gentleness, faithfulness, and self-control—that kind of "born from above" stuff.

Most of God's children *are* religious. Some are *very* religious. But not everyone who's religious is one of His children. You need to be born again. You need to be born "from above."

Open your heart. Ask God to make you one of His children. Ask Jesus to fill you with His Spirit. It's not too late to start over. Just ask Nicodemus. You're never too old to become a brand-new child of God! That's God's Word for you today.

God wants children after His own heart who are seeking to become like Him.

70

DO YOU WANT TO GET WELL?

JOHN 5:1–9

***When Jesus saw him lying there and learned
that he had been in this condition for a long time,
he asked him, "Do you want to get well?"***
(John 5:6 NIV)

Jesus sometimes asked questions that seem silly—like this one: "Do you want to get well?" The man had been an invalid for thirty-eight years. Of course he wanted to get well! Or so you would think. Sometimes people don't. Sometimes, as hard as their lives might seem, it's all they know.

I read about a man some years ago who robbed a bank and then waited outside for the police. He had recently been released from prison after serving twenty years. But being out, he discovered, was harder than being in. So he robbed a bank to go back. Prison may be a place with bars and a cell and armed guards and limited freedom, but it was *familiar.* So he went back.

Sometimes you'll scratch your head at people like this. You'll help people out of circumstances that you would certainly think they wouldn't want to be in, but they go back. They go back to the drugs, the alcohol, the abusive spouse, or whatever unhealthy place they've been in.

Now before we pass judgment too quickly, let's just be honest. It's hard. As difficult as all those things are, change is sometimes even harder. You have to learn how not to be a victim. You have to walk away from friends who help you stay addicted. You have to learn how to cope with the pain you've been medicating and hiding from. You have to be willing to take responsibility for your life rather than blaming everyone else. It's easier to say, "I can't," than to say "With God's help, I *will.*"

So the man Jesus talked to had to make a choice. Did he walk again, learn a trade, and enter into a life that was totally unfamiliar to him? Or did he stay an invalid and get by the way he had up to that point? The answer is sometimes harder than we think.

Let me ask you: Do *you* want to be well? I want to warn you that the new way won't be easier than the old one. It will be *better* and *healthier,* but not necessarily easier. Jesus can heal you. He can deliver you. He can help you walk away from the life you now have that you hate.

But before He can do any of those things, He needs to know—"Do you *want* to be well?" Are you willing to stop blaming? Are you willing to stop playing the victim? Are you willing to go through the hard work of learning a different path or making new friends? Are you willing to let go of what's familiar to take hold of something that is scary, unknown, and new?

If you want to be well, Jesus can help you. Reach out to Him right now. He *wants* to help you. He wants to see you walk in the freedom and joy that you were created to have. He wants to give you the life that up until now you have only imagined.

But before He can do that for you, you have to do something for yourself. You have to actually *want* to be well. God has put the key to freedom in your hands. He's ready when you are. That's God's Word for you today.

> ***Jesus can help you walk away from the
> life you now have that you hate.***

71

BELIEVING ON THE INSIDE

Despite all the miraculous signs Jesus had done,
most of the people still did not believe in him.
(John 12:37)

In February 2015 fourteen-year-old John Smith fell through the ice and was submerged underwater for fifteen minutes. The paramedics arrived and began CPR. They worked on him all the way to the hospital, where the doctors and nurses took over. After forty-five minutes of trying to revive him with no results, his mother, Joyce, was invited into the room and was asked how long they should continue. As she walked into the room she began praying loudly for God to bring life back to her son's lifeless body.

Suddenly Dr. Kent Sutterer, the attending physician, shouted, "We've got a pulse! We've got a pulse!" Everyone was stunned. However, even though the boy's heart had started again, a brain without oxygen for even half that amount of time would leave a person in a total vegetative state. But John walked out of the hospital a few weeks later with no signs of damage at all!

The kid had been "dead" for forty-five minutes, and now, following his mother's prayer, he is perfectly fine. How do you explain that? The doctor called it a "bona fide miracle." That's a term doctors don't throw around too often.

Some people wouldn't call it a miracle, claiming the kid was just "lucky." Others would say his heart was actually still beating but just really, really slowly. Many people would find a lot of other ways to try to explain the event, but a "miracle" wouldn't be one of them. Even in the face of the facts—fifteen minutes underwater, no heartbeat detected by experienced health professionals, reviving *immediately* following the prayer and no lingering brain or physical damage—some people wouldn't accept a supernatural explanation. That's because they don't *want* to believe.

To admit to a miracle is to admit the divine. To admit the divine means there's a God to whom we have to answer. Many just can't do that. They couldn't admit it about Jesus in spite of the numerous miracles that He performed. And they can't admit it today.

So don't get discouraged when friends or family of yours don't believe. And don't get mad because you want God to do something miraculous that would just make it impossible for them not to believe. It most likely wouldn't matter. Jesus showed us that the miracles often don't make that much of a difference. People don't believe simply because something miraculous happens around them. People believe when something miraculous happens *within* them. A spiritual eye is opened. A cold heart gets softened. A dead spirit gets awakened.

Miracles can often boost our faith, but they don't usually cause it to happen initially. So if you've been asking God to show a miracle to someone who doesn't believe, ask Him to make it a miracle on the *inside*. Because believing on the inside is something many people have to do before they can believe on the outside—even when a fourteen-year-old who's been dead for forty-five minutes comes back to life. That's God's Word for you today.

> **People believe when something miraculous happens within them.**

72

FAITH IN THOSE MOMENTS

JOHN 20:24–29

Then he said to Thomas, "Put your finger here; see my hands. Reach out your hand and put it into my side. Stop doubting and believe." Thomas said to him, "My Lord and my God!" Then Jesus told him, "Because you have seen me, you have believed; blessed are those who have not seen and yet have believed."
(John 20:27–29 NIV)

"Doubting Thomas"—what a great way to be remembered! Even people who don't know the story have heard of the nickname. How come the rest of the crew didn't get a moniker like that?—like "Cowardly Peter" or "John the Brown-Noser"? I mean, they all had some pretty glaring flaws. But Thomas gets immortalized for doubting.

Who can blame him for doubting? He saw Jesus die. It was a brutal, horrible, stomach-turning death. He knew Jesus was buried and gone. Sure, Jesus said that He would rise again, but who can hold on to such a promise in the face of reality? Someone with faith! And that's what Jesus was getting at with Thomas. Of course, Thomas believed now. He could *see* Jesus. He could *touch* Jesus. He could *hear* Jesus. *Anyone* can believe when they can do those things! It's the believing *without* those things that's hard. Jesus gave people like that another name: "blessed."

I was having a conversation on this very topic with a woman in my office today. We were talking about how we have this intuitive sense that there is a God even when we aren't sure who exactly He is. There are those times when He shows up in incredible and wonderful ways and almost takes our breaths away with what He does. We talked about how we have to hold onto those moments—because other moments are coming, moments when God *doesn't* show up and save the day, moments when He doesn't answer the prayer the way we want, moments when His silence is absolutely deafening.

It's in those moments that we find it hard to believe. But it's in those moments that we most *need* to believe! Because it's in those awful, foreboding moments that our hearts are looking and longing for something to hang onto. If we can find faith in those moments, we can make it through. We will be *blessed.*

Maybe you are in one of those moments now. Maybe you're in a moment where it seems God is dead and buried, or at least totally hidden from your view. Maybe you've lost hope, lost faith, lost your footing, and are in need of a sure place to stand. Reach out your hand and your heart to Him. Ask Jesus to make Himself present so you can *see* Him, *feel* Him, and *touch* Him.

It's okay. Sometimes we all find ourselves a bit of a "Doubting Thomas." But as He does restore your faith, mark this moment. Seal it in your heart and mind. Burn it in your soul as it surely burned into Thomas's that day. Because somewhere down the road you'll need this faith again. You'll need Jesus to be real again. And if you can remember *this moment* while you're experiencing *that moment,* then He'll be as real and alive in your heart as He is right now.

Then your doubt, your fear, and your anxiety will all give way to faith. And you will be one of those Jesus calls *blessed.* That's God's Word for you today.

> **Ask Jesus to make Himself present so you can
> see Him, feel Him, and touch Him.**

73

THE COURAGE TO PRAY FOR COURAGE

ACTS 4:1–31

"And now, O Lord, hear their threats,
and give us, your servants, great boldness in preaching
your word." . . . After this prayer, the meeting place shook,
and they were all filled with the Holy Spirit. Then they
preached the word of God with boldness.
(Acts 4:29, 31)

You can learn a lot about people by listening to how they pray. Some people ask God for blessing. They want their homes to be better, their jobs to be better, their lives to be better. And they want God to do all the heavy lifting! Some people pray and ask God to make the world the way they think it ought to be—you know, their candidate in office, the right weather for their activity, and that person they're arguing with to come to their senses and see it their way. A lot of people pray for life to be easier. They ask for less pressure, less resistance, and less hassle from people making their lives difficult.

But look at how the disciples prayed. After getting arrested for preaching about Jesus and knowing that even more persecution was on its way, they didn't pray for their lives to be better. They didn't ask for things to go their way. They didn't pray for things to be any easier. They prayed that God would help them be brave. They prayed for *courage*. And God gave it to them!

This is such a revolutionary understanding for us. We don't get that most of the time it's not the world around us or the people around us that God most wants to change. It's *us*! We keep asking God to fix stuff. He wants to fix *us*. We keep asking God for a life that's easier. God wants to make us stronger instead.

The disciples knew that the pushback they had just received was just the beginning. Soon there would be wave after wave of persecution. If God made this first wave easy, they wouldn't be prepared for the next wave. So they didn't ask for "easy." They had the courage to ask for *courage*. God answering *that* prayer would make them *strong!*

What do *you* pray for? Have you found yourself getting frustrated with God because He hasn't been giving you what you've been asking for? Maybe it's because you've been praying for the wrong thing. Maybe you've been praying for God to change these people all around you while what God really wants to do is to change your heart toward them. Maybe you've been praying for God to bless you while what God really wants to do is to help you learn how to be grateful for what you have. Maybe you've been praying for God to make your life easier while what God really wants to do is to make you *strong*.

Maybe you'll get more positive answers if you pray for the right stuff! Stop looking for the easier way and ask God to help you grow up a bit. Have the courage to pray for courage. Then maybe God will do something *in* you and *through* you that He's never done before. And maybe you'll begin to become that person you've always wanted to be. That's God's Word for you today.

> ***Don't pray for God to make your life easy. Pray for Him to make you strong.***

74

A MONUMENT TO OUR MESS

ACT 8:1–4

*A great wave of persecution began that day,
sweeping over the church in Jerusalem; and all the
believers except the apostles were scattered through
the regions of Judea and Samaria. . . . But the believers
who were scattered preached the Good News
about Jesus wherever they went.*
(Acts 8:1, 4)

In Enterprise, Alabama, is found a statue to a hero, a hero that singlehandedly caused the state to flourish. This hero was not a general or an officer in the army. He was not a doctor or medical research expert. He was not an entrepreneur, a businessman, or an inventor. In fact, this hero was not even human. It was a beetle called the "boll weevil."

In 1915 the boll weevil began migrating into Alabama, coming up from Mexico. By 1918 it was destroying entire crops of cotton, which was the backbone of Alabama's source of income. In response to the boll weevil, a man named H. M. Sessions secured some financing and introduced growing the peanut there. The end result was that the farmers learned how to diversify their crops, and they began thriving again. On December 11, 1919, a monument to the boll weevil was erected at the corner of College and Main. The inscription reads, "In profound appreciation of the boll weevil and what it has done as the herald of prosperity, this monument was erected by the citizens of Enterprise, Coffee County, Alabama." What they had thought was devastation became the best thing to happen to their economy.

That's what God did in our passage today. The rising dislike of these Jesus followers gave way to an all-out persecution. People were arrested. Families were split apart. Many were killed. It was one of the darkest moments in Christian history. But in the midst of this persecution something happened. The people scattered. Though they had been primarily centered in Jerusalem, they now fled everywhere. And they took with them this gospel that had so changed their lives. The religious leaders persecuting them had hoped to squash this rising new faith in Jesus. But instead, these Christ followers now had *new* audiences and places to share what Jesus had done. The church up until this time had been strong. Now it became *unstoppable*. In hindsight perhaps they should have erected a statue to these persecutors!

God is wonderfully at work in our darkest moments. He is amazing at taking our setbacks, our disasters, our "boll weevil" moments and doing something *incredible*. He is not only the God who created something out of nothing. He is the God who can make the magnificent out of a mess!

So bring Him your mess, whatever your mess may be. When life stomps on you, don't you believe for a moment that it's over. It's not. It's just a new beginning.

Who knows? Maybe one day you'll look back and feel like building a monument to the "boll weevil" that devastated *you*. Sometimes our messes have just the right ingredients for God to work a miracle! That's God's Word for you today.

When life stomps on you, it's not over.
It's just a new beginning.

75

ARE WE THERE YET?

ROMANS 4:18–22

Abraham never wavered in believing God's promise. In fact, his faith grew stronger, and in this he brought glory to God. He was fully convinced that God is able to do whatever he promises.
(Romans 4:20–21)

I have a confession to make: I'm not good at waiting. I don't like sitting in a doctor's office waiting room. I'm not a fan of long lines at restaurants. And I despise sitting in stand-still traffic. I guess I'm not really good at *any* form of delayed gratification. I want to be there *now.* I want to have it *now.* I want to eat *now.*

I'm that way with God too. When I feel that God has promised something to me or led me in a particular direction,

I'm asking, "Are we there yet?" Even though in my head I know God has details to work out and that there is shaping in me He needs to do, it doesn't matter. I want to put the pedal to the metal and *get there*—we can take care of the particulars later. But it's the particulars that are most important to God.

That's why I think Abraham was one of God's favorites. I have to be honest: when I was reading this verse about Abraham today, I was embarrassed. I am the antithesis of this! Abraham was seventy-five years old when God promised him that he would be "the father of nations." God wouldn't fulfill that promise until Abraham was one hundred. That's twenty-five years of being in "the waiting room"! That's twenty-five years of long delays and "When's it going to happen?" kinds of thoughts. That's twenty-five years of asking, "Did I hear this right?"

But instead of Abraham's faith growing weaker, it grew stronger. That meant he believed God more at one hundred than he did at seventy-five—even though he had endured twenty-five years of God not coming through! Maybe that's why, four thousand years later, we're still talking about Abraham's faith. They won't be talking about mine even *four weeks* from now!

Abraham believed God. Do you? Have you felt as if God hasn't come through for you the way He said He would? Have you felt as if you've lived up to your end of the bargain and

God's hedging on His? Do you feel as if you've been in God's "waiting room" for a while now? Are you growing a bit antsy and frustrated?

I get it. I'm wired like that too. But let's both learn something from Abraham today: God *will* come through! Instead of waking up every day and wondering why it hasn't happened, let's wake up knowing that we are *one day closer* to God showing up! Let's look and listen for those "particulars" that God is trying to show us and shape us with so we can be ready for God when God is ready for us.

Paul says that Abraham brought glory to God with his faith. Let's you and I do that. Let's give God more glory and less grief. We can trust God. He will let us know when we get there. That's God's Word for you today.

***Have you felt as if God hasn't come through
for you the way He said He would?***

76

GORILLA GLUE LOVE

I am convinced that nothing can ever separate us from God's love. Neither death nor life, neither angels nor demons, neither our fears for today nor our worries about tomorrow—not even the powers of hell can separate us from God's love. No power in the sky above or in the earth below—indeed, nothing in all creation will ever be able to separate us from the love of God that is revealed in Christ Jesus our Lord. **(Romans 8:38–39)**

Nothing can ever separate you from God's love. He loves you in spite of what you've done. No matter how awful it may seem to you, He still loves you. It doesn't matter how many times you've done it. He still loves you. It doesn't matter how others feel about what you've done. They may call you an outcast, a degenerate, or a criminal. They may disown you, reject you, abandon you, refuse to speak to you, or hate you. But God still loves you.

His love is not based on your performance—past, present, or future. His love is not even contingent on your love for Him. You may be mad at Him, confused by Him, or even believe that He doesn't exist. But even your harshest feelings or total apathy toward Him can't separate you from how much He loves you.

Other people can't separate you from God's love. You may be an orphan, abandoned by your family. But God still thinks of you as one of His precious children, and He loves you. You may be divorced and have been made to feel that you're a failure, unwanted, unworthy. But God loves you. You may have been abused or neglected as a child. You may have grown up all your life feeling that you were "broken," "damaged goods," or just "property" to be treated however someone wanted. But you are precious, priceless, and perfect to God. And He loves you. You may have been that one with the lying smile, the one who always made everyone believe that you had it all together. No one ever knew how much you really hated yourself. But God knew. And He loves you.

Judgmental pastors and church leaders can't separate you from God's love. Rude religious people who always feel they get to speak on God's behalf can't separate you from God's love. Your problems haven't separated you from God's love. Your doubts haven't separated you from God's love. Your fears, your struggles, your worries, your hidden pain—none of it can separate you from God's love. God's love is reaching out to you right now wherever you are. He is screaming, "I love you!" in a thousand different ways. No matter what any other voices may be telling you or what tapes may be playing in your head, Paul wrote this down so you would never forget— and God asked me to write it to you today.

Nothing can ever separate you from His love. Nothing. Not ever. That's God's Word for you today.

God's love is reaching out to you right now wherever you are.

77

THE GRAND PAUSE

*The message of the cross is foolish to those
who are headed for destruction! But we who are being
saved know it is the very power of God.*
(1 Corinthians 1:18)

You have to admit—the cross doesn't make sense to someone who doesn't understand or believe. It didn't make sense to the people in Jesus's day, and it doesn't make sense to them today. Think about it. Many of us Christians wear a symbol of torture, death, and humiliation around our necks. Criminals, not kings, died on crosses. The worst of the worst were put to death like that, not the best of the best. Crucifixion was the end of the line for thieves and murderers. You build monuments to heroes and holy people, not hang them on crosses. What's so special about one more powerless man hanging there lifeless and nailed to a tree? That's why people think it's so foolish. It doesn't make sense—that is, unless you know the rest of the story!

Jesus wasn't murdered, at least not against His will. They didn't take His life—He *gave* it. He had the power to walk away or to destroy those who took Him captive. But He didn't. This wasn't a man hanging powerless on a tree. This was God in the flesh demonstrating the depths of His love. He didn't die begging for mercy or cursing His perpetrators. He died asking His Father to forgive them for their foolishness. How could they know that this wasn't some random act? How could they guess that this was actually the plan before humanity was created? How could they understand that this was the farthest thing from the end of the line for Jesus's ministry?

This wasn't the end—it was simply the grand pause before the finale. We call it *the Resurrection.* Soon God's symphony would be complete, the power of God would be revealed, and all that had been thought lost would be reclaimed. The cross became the emblem that represented the fact that when life is at its worst, God is at His best! It's a power we live in and claim today.

Maybe you're at a "cross" moment yourself. Maybe things have turned out very differently than you had hoped, and maybe you're feeling as if much of what you've dreamed has been nailed to a tree. Yet in spite of your setbacks, hurts, and disappointments, you find yourself strangely encouraged today. That's because it is not a man on a cross who lives within you but rather a risen Savior! Something is telling you that in spite of it all you will be just fine or maybe even *better* on the other side of this. So you smile. Your hope in that power within you is greater than the pain of discouragement.

Some around you won't understand. Some will say you're a bit loony to be this happy when so much is going wrong. Some will even say you're living in denial. That's because the cross doesn't make sense to them. They think the song is over.

But you know it's just a grand pause. God has more music yet to play. You *will* live again. On to the finale! That's God's Word for you today!

> **The cross represents the fact that when life is at its worst, God is at His best.**

78

TIME TO GROW UP

*When I was a child, I spoke and thought
and reasoned as a child. But when I grew up,
I put away childish things.*
(1 Corinthians 13:11)

1 Corinthians 13 is one of the most beautiful chapters
in the entire Bible. It is one that's quoted at many
weddings. As he sums up his beautiful thoughts on love, Paul
makes a striking and powerful statement that we should all
take to heart: *It's time to grow up.* Do you have any idea of how
much doing just that would help our marriages, our homes,
our churches, and our work places?

Think about it: what if we actually took responsibility for
what we said, what we did, or when we messed up—instead

of passing the blame on to someone else? How many times have you heard a kid say, "It's not *my* fault!"? But it *is*. And we all know it is. You only make yourself look childish by not accepting your guilt. Or how about finally realizing that you don't always get your way? Isn't it ridiculous how some people when they can't have it their way will sulk, stew, pout, or just be nasty to everyone? It's an adult version of a temper tantrum. And it's childish.

Growing up means we learn that the universe doesn't really revolve around us. Lots of other people have ideas, needs, and desires, and they're important too. Growing up means we learn to listen rather than having to prove our point. Growing up means we learn to let others go first. Growing up means we look for the "greater good" and not what always may simply be good for us.

Earlier in this chapter of 1 Corinthians Paul said that love is "patient and kind . . . not jealous or boastful or proud or rude. It does not demand its own way. . . . It keeps no record of being wronged" (vv. 4–5). That's a *grown-up* love! Growing up means we lose the pettiness, lose the whining, lose giving others the silent treatment. Growing up means we realize how precious relationships really are. We're willing to *go first* in saying, "I'm sorry," if it'll help get us back to where we need to be with each other. Kids take their toys and go home. Adults sit down and work things out.

I want to challenge you to go back and reread 1 Corinthians 13 with fresh eyes. As you read it, ask God this personal and very important question: *Where in my relationships with others am I still acting like a child?* Maybe it's time to let go of some of those old ways of thinking, talking, and acting. Maybe it's time to let go of the "kid" in you that is causing you so many problems and to become more of the man or woman you know you need to be. Maybe it's time to stop blaming, pouting, whining, and complaining.

When we do that, we can then love the way Paul challenged us to. Love, real love, isn't easy. It takes doing something that most of us really don't want to do: grow up. That's God's Word for you today.

Growing up means we learn that the universe doesn't really revolve around us!

79

THE GIFT THAT KEEPS ON GIVING

*All praise to God, the Father of our
Lord Jesus Christ. God is our merciful Father
and the source of all comfort. He comforts us in all
our troubles, so that we can comfort others. When they
are troubled, we will be able to give them the
same comfort God has given us.*
(2 Corinthians 1:3–4)

Several years ago in ministry I came to terms with some
pain I had never faced. It had to do with my family
while I was growing up. When the emotional dam inside me
broke, it came pouring out in an almost unstoppable flood. It
felt as if my emotions were out of control, as if I were having
some kind of "breakdown." I went to a counselor and spent

the next six months talking through my past. I did a lot of grieving. Some sessions I simply wept and said very little. It was wonderfully cleansing. My counselor guided me through it, and I discovered that God could heal not only our bodies but also our damaged emotions. I've often told pastors and leaders that my time in counseling was the best gift I have ever given to my family, my church, and myself. But it's also been a gift from God that has kept on giving.

Recently I've been able to come alongside another pastor who is going through similar territory. He is about the age I was when I went through my tough stuff. When he told me about what he was experiencing, I shared what I went through, talking about the fears, the feelings of being out of control, and the surreal nature of telling myself to pull myself together but having absolutely no ability to do so. More than once he exclaimed, "Yes! That's it!" Hearing the voice of someone else who had been down that dark path and had emerged was wonderfully comforting for him. We've talked several times since then. I'm not his counselor or therapist, and I don't try to be that for him. I'm just passing on the gift that God gave me so many years ago. I'm simply comforting him with the same comfort that God gave to me.

This is an important point that Paul makes about suffering in today's scripture. We often ask God, "Why?" when we're going through difficult times. We assume that there must be some lesson in it for us that we need to learn. And there always is.

But I want to suggest that our difficult times are not just about *us*. They are also about all those others we will meet along the way on the journey. They are the people who need a guide to help them find their way through their difficult places. God allowed us to go through ours so we could help them go through theirs.

So if you're in one of those tough places today, I feel for you. I hope you find a good guide, friend, counselor, or pastor to walk with you as you find your way. Take heart. God *will* see you through. But take good notes. My guess is that down the road you will have the opportunity to be a guide for someone else. The gift that God gives to you through a good friend or counselor and His loving, healing presence will keep on giving *through* you. Then the circle will be complete and you will know your "why." That's God's Word for you today.

God allows us to go through our troubles so we can help others go through theirs.

80

THE DIFFERENCE IN IN THE FRUIT

The Holy Spirit produces this kind of fruit in our lives: love, joy, peace, patience, kindness, goodness, faithfulness, gentleness, and self-control.
(Galatians 5:22–23)

Some years ago a friend of mine called me, distraught and confused by a Christian leader at his church who was making decisions that were causing considerable division and hurt. But more concerning was the leader's attitude—he was arrogant, uncaring, and unapproachable. My friend said, "I'm so confused. I don't know what to think about all of this because he seems to be such a godly leader."

I said, "Godly? What do you mean by 'godly'?"

"Well, he quotes a lot of scripture, says he's prayed about things, and tells us he hears from God."

I responded: "Let me give you some words: *Love, joy, peace, patience, kindness, goodness, faithfulness, gentleness, self-control.* Do these describe this guy?"

Laughing, he replied, "No, *definitely* not!"

"Then this leader isn't really godly," I explained. "He's just *religious.*"

People mix up these two terms all the time. Being "religious" has to do with the stuff you *do.* You go to church. You say prayers. You memorize Bible verses. You speak in fluent King James English. You act very "holy."

Being godly, on the other hand, has to do with who you *are.* You care about people. You're compassionate and kind. You don't flex your muscles of power simply because you can. You make people wish they were more like you rather than making them despise you. The "fruit" of your life is obvious to people. It flows out of your heart.

The "religious" people of the world are scary. They tend to justify doing stuff the rest of us find reprehensible. And they do it in the name of God! In Matthew 23 Jesus called these kinds of people "snakes." He said to beware of them—and certainly not to be like them!

Paul said that when we really lean into God there will be some pretty incredible fruit coming out in our lives. That list is probably worth another read: *Love, joy, peace, patience, kindness, goodness, faithfulness, gentleness, self-control.* Which of those do you think people see coming out in *you*? Which of those do you think you should spend a little time with God asking Him to help you produce?

Trust me: your home, your office, your school, and your community really don't need one more "religious" person. But they could definitely use a few more *godly* ones. The world doesn't need more people who quote the Bible. They need more people who act like its Author. The difference is in The Fruit. That's God's Word for you today.

> **The world doesn't need people
> who quote the Bible. They need people
> who act like its Author.**

81

LOVED BEFORE YOU WERE BORN

*Even before he made the world, God loved us
and chose us in Christ to be holy and without fault
in his eyes. God decided in advance to adopt us into
his own family by bringing us to himself through
Jesus Christ. This is what he wanted to do, and it
gave him great pleasure.*
(Ephesians 1:4–5)

I admit it—I'm a hopeless romantic. I love romantic movies, heroes who save the woman in distress, and happy endings. I especially love romantic music. There's a great old Savage Garden song that is one of my favorites called "I Knew I Loved You," in which the singer tells about loving someone he hasn't even met yet. I love the thought of that. It's as if you're in love with the idea of who the person is, and then (cue the fireworks) you *meet* the person—who is even more wonderful than you imagined! Now *that's* love!

I think God's a bit of a hopeless romantic like me. Think about it. God was in the process of creating the world. As He thought about what He would make and how He would make it, He came up with this incredible idea: *you*. He thought about every wonderful, unique part of you. The more He thought about who you would be, the more in love with you He fell. Oh, He knew you would play hard-to-get. He knew you would try to do life all on your own, even though He made you to need Him.

So He also came up with a plan to win your heart. That plan was Jesus. In that moment when you realized there was something missing in your life, Jesus would be there to let you know that it was God. When you opened your heart to Him, it was even better than God imagined it would be at the beginning of time. The *reality* of your returning His love was even better than the *idea* of it! It gave Him "great pleasure." God knew He loved you before He met you. In fact, He knew it before He even *made* you. He couldn't wait for the day when you would return that love.

So I hope you feel special today. I hope you feel like the incredible treasure and unbelievable "catch" that you were created to be. No matter where life has taken you or what life has done to you, you are still a dream-come-true to God. He not only loved you from the moment you were born into this world, but He also loved you before this world was even born! You are more special to Him than He even imagined you would be—so special, in fact, that His plan from the beginning was that He would come to earth Himself to reclaim you, even though it meant leaving heaven and going through hell to do so. To Him you were worth it.

And you *still* are. I know it's sappy, but that's how love is. And it's how God feels about *you*! That's God's Word for you today.

> **God knew He loved you before He met you.**
> **He knew it before He even made *you*!**

82

ONE PERSON'S TRASH IS ANOTHER PERSON'S TREASURE

God saved you by his grace when you believed.
And you can't take credit for this; it is a gift from God.
Salvation is not a reward for the good things we have
done, so none of us can boast about it. For we are God's
masterpiece. He has created us anew in Christ Jesus, so we
can do the good things he planned for us long ago.
(Ephesians 2:8–10)

Michelle Reader is an artist. She has a unique imagination that makes her special among those in her field. As she matured as an artist, she began developing a passion for 3-D art. So she began making sculptures. But unlike most sculptors, who make their images out of granite or marble or some other type of stone, Michelle specializes in utilizing unique materials. She makes her sculptures out of *trash*. That's right. She digs through dumpsters, checks out junkyards, and sorts through recycling centers looking for the materials from which to make works of art valued at thousands of dollars. In her hands what was once one person's trash literally becomes another person's treasure.

Paul reminds us that this is what God does as well. We sometimes totally trash our lives. We make choices and choose lifestyles that can leave us broken, beaten up, battered, and cast aside. We may be just a shell of our former selves. We may have had others tell us that we're valueless. Some of us have even been called "trash."

But God sees something that others don't see. In His magnificent imagination God sees something worth *saving,* something worth *preserving,* something worth *restoring.* So God climbs into the dumpsters of our lives and pulls us out. By His amazing grace He brings beauty, value, and usefulness back to us. Others may call us a "mess"—God calls us His "masterpiece."

So take a look in the mirror. Do you know what you are? You're a work of art. You're a living, breathing sculpture carved by the hand of God. It doesn't matter how soiled your life may have become. It doesn't matter how low you've sunk, what you've done, or how long you've been in a heap on the side of the road. It doesn't matter how many people have given up on you or washed you out of their lives.

God sees your beauty. God sees your potential. God sees the incredible life that grace can make out of your mess. And if others try to remind you of who you used to be and try to put you back in the landfill of your past, don't listen to them. Listen to the Artist. He'll remind you that another person's trash is His own precious treasure. *You* are His masterpiece! That's God's Word for you today.

You're a living, breathing sculpture
carved by the hand of God.

83

WHO ARE YOU IMITATING?

Imitate God, therefore, in everything you do,
because you are his dear children. Live a life filled
with love, following the example of Christ.
(Ephesians 5:1–2)

Not long ago we were looking through some photographs of our grandkids and I spotted one that was really cute. It was a picture of my grandson, Maddox, following me around the yard. I was cutting the grass, and he was dutifully walking behind me pushing his little plastic mower.

As I looked at it I suddenly flashed back about thirty years to when my son Ben, Maddox's father, was a child. He used to do that very same thing! He loved to try to do whatever

I was doing. So when I cut the grass, he would bust out his little mower and follow along. I laughed as I thought about it. I also wondered if Maddox would lose his zeal for cutting grass by the time he became a teen as Ben did. Somehow doing it for real wasn't as fun as following me around pretending!

It's the nature of children to imitate their parents, whether it's for good or bad. What we say they say. What we do they do. There is an instinctive nature within them to want to be like us. They watch *us* to figure out how *they're* supposed to act in the world. It's how we're designed to be.

Our passage today reminds us that God has designed it to be that way with Him as well. He is our Father, and we are His children. His Spirit lives within us, and we instinctively want to be like Him. So how do we learn to act in this world now that we have this new nature within us? Paul says we *imitate* God. We look at Jesus, who was the living, breathing, visual image of God, and we live as He lived. We act as He acted. We talk as He talked. As we look at His life and how He lived among us, we get behind our little mowers and seek to follow Him.

Oh, we don't do it perfectly. We sometimes take our cues more from the neighbor boy or girl down the street, who's a bit of brat, than we do from our Father. But if we can keep ourselves focused on our Father, He'll show us how to be, what to do, and how to talk. The longer we do it the more it becomes a part of who we are. That's called "growing up."

So who are you imitating? Think back over the past week and consider how you acted, what you did, and how you spoke to others. Does it remind you of God? Were you living in a way that was imitating your heavenly Father, or was your behavior more of an imitation of some of the bratty people who live around you?

It's not easy growing up. Part of the deal is that you have to choose who you're going to be like. Listen to the Spirit whom God has put within you. You are His child, recreated in His image, to be like Him. Renew your commitment to focus your attention back on Jesus. Live your life as *He* would live your life.

And don't do it just for you. Do it for all those little ones with mowers who are following you! That's God's Word for you today.

It's not easy growing up.
You have to choose who you're going to be like.

84

THE DEATH OF A THOUSAND CUTS

Do everything without complaining and arguing.
(Philippians 2:14)

About a thousand years ago in Imperial China a form of torture/execution called "lingchi" was used. It was also known as "the death of a thousand cuts." Though applied in many different ways, the basic idea was to simply make small incisions over a period of time, causing the death of an individual to be long and drawn out rather than swift. Depending on the procedure, death could take anywhere from hours to days, coming only after incredible suffering. This form of execution was eventually outlawed by the Qing dynasty in 1905.

I would suggest to you that many of us are still applying the barbaric practice today. Only we do it with our *words* instead of our knives. It' slowly killing people—some of whom we say we love!

Most pastors don't leave their churches because of big problems. They leave because of discouragement caused by the constant complaining of usually no more than six to ten people or so. I told someone once that ministry isn't learning how to take on the "big dogs." It's more like learning how to run a marathon while a pack of Chihuahuas nip at your ankles!

Most spouses don't leave each other because of major issues in the relationship. Usually a husband or wife just gets tired of never being able to "do anything right" or the way that it's "supposed to be done." The snide remarks, the little barbs, and the harsh responses bleed the relationship dry until there's no life or love left. Often when the depleted partner finally leaves, the other spouse is still clueless as to why they left, totally unaware that their words, tone, and expressions were like little razors slicing their partner's heart.

We do the same to our kids. Then we wonder how they grew up to be such angry, cynical and critical adults. Employees leave companies because of the same reason. Have you ever had a boss who rarely compliments you when you excel but never fails to point out your mistakes? Ever had one who finds a flaw in everything you do and thinks every idea you have is a dumb one? Nick, nick, nick. Hurt, hurt, hurt. Wound, wound, wound. It's not the big things that are killing us—we bleed to death from the thousand "cuts."

I have a challenge for you. I want you to commit today's verse to memory and recite it every day for a week. Then I want you to ask God to help you think of someone whom maybe you complain to or argue with more than you should. For one week don't complain or argue at all. Affirm the person. Compliment the person. Tell the person how utterly awesome they are, even if for no other reason than putting up with *you*! For one week become the person's biggest fan, their biggest supporter and greatest encourager.

Do that, and I feel sure that after only one week you'll begin to see a different pastor, a different spouse, a different child, or a different employee. People come alive when they are affirmed and valued. It's like receiving a relationship transfusion.

Be a life-*giver* this week and not a life-*taker*. "Do everything without complaining and arguing." It may be the greatest gift you ever give to those you love. That's God's Word for you today.

> *People come alive when they are affirmed and valued. It's like a relationship transfusion!*

85

HAVE A NICE FLIGHT!

*Don't worry about anything; instead,
pray about everything. Tell God what you need,
and thank him for all he has done. Then you will
experience God's peace, which exceeds anything we
can understand. His peace will guard your hearts
and minds as you live in Christ Jesus.*
(Philippians 4:6–7)

Several years ago I had a really bad experience flying. We took off in a storm in a small forty-passenger plane. During our ascent we hit an air pocket and the plane just dropped out of the sky. For a few intense seconds I thought I was going to die. Obviously I didn't.

But after that event I developed panic attacks whenever I had to fly. They would start a few days before I actually flew. When it came time to take off, I would grip the armrests, perform rituals I hoped would protect me, and then jump at every bump of air we encountered. That continued for a couple of years.

Then one day on a plane as I started my pre-flight ritual, God reminded me of a verse: "Who of you by worrying can add a single hour to your life?" (Luke 12:25 NIV). Suddenly I had a thought I had never thought before: Worrying about the plane going down would *not* keep it in the air. In fact, all it was doing was robbing me of enjoying the journey. God used that simple understanding to heal me. I was trying to control something I had no ability to control. Trying to do that is not only silly—it is self-destructive!

Paul gives us some great advice about worry: Stop it. But he also gives some good follow-up instructions about what to do instead. The first thing he says is *pray.* What a great idea! Worry is essentially praying to *ourselves.* We're trying to figure out how to take care of that thing we have no power over as if *we're* God. But we're not. So let's actually give it to God! *He does* have power over it!

Then, after putting the uncontrollable in the hands of the One who has control, we're told to do something else: thank God for what He's already done. Doing that takes our minds off what we're afraid *might* happen and puts them on the incredible blessings that have *already* happened. The result of doing those two things, Paul says, fills our minds and our hearts with *peace*. And isn't that what worry is looking for all along?

So what uncontrollable thing are you trying to control? What's keeping you up at night, making your heart pound with anxiety or freezing your mind with fear? Your worry isn't fixing anything—it's only stealing from you. All that anxiety about the future is robbing you of the precious moments we call *today.* It's keeping you from enjoying the journey and it's time to stop.

Give your uncontrollable problem to the One who has hands big enough to hold it. Then do something else. Begin thanking Him. Thank Him for all the blessings of your life, naming each one. Thank Him for all the answers to prayer you've experienced through the years, and affirm His faithfulness. Let what He has already done give you the assurance of what He's *going* to do.

"Praying to yourself" by worrying fills your life with panic. Praying to God fills your life with peace. Take it from a guy who figured out he couldn't keep a plane in the sky no matter how hard he worried. Peace is better. Have a nice flight. That's God's Word for you today.

Give your uncontrollable problem to the One who has hands big enough to hold it.

86

STANDING TALL WHEN OTHERS FALL

*Just as you accepted Christ Jesus as your Lord,
you must continue to follow him. Let your roots grow
down into him, and let your lives be built on him. Then
your faith will grow strong in the truth you were taught,
and you will overflow with thankfulness.*
(Colossians 2:6–7)

I remember my first trip to Colorado. For a kid who grew up in the Midwest, the majestic, scenic views were almost surreal. The beauty of the mountains absolutely took my breath away. But as we made our way up the switchbacks, I noticed there seemed to be a lot of very tall trees that had fallen over. When I asked why these seemingly huge, strong trees would just fall over like that, the answer was simple:

Shallow roots. If the soil was too rocky or the roots didn't get to interlock with other tree roots, the trees couldn't stand in the mountain winds. No matter how healthy they looked above ground, it was the roots that were the real source of strength.

That's true for us as well. Many people really don't take the time or make the effort to make their roots go deep in God. For a lot of us the depth of our faith is the occasional worship service, a little Christian music while we drive, and the family prayer over dinner. All are good things. They just don't take us very deep with God. As long as life doesn't hit us with any "high winds," we seem to get by. But then the winds do come and you get hit with that financial setback. Or you encounter a gust of bad news from your doctor. Or you ride out a storm of relational difficulty. That's when you find out how deep your roots of faith go! Can your faith endure those kinds of winds? That's when many people fall apart.

I regularly challenge our people to develop habits of getting into God's Word daily, even if it's only for five to fifteen minutes a day. Why? Our faith roots need it! I tell our people they need to be in classes and groups where they are connecting and sharing their journey with other believers. Why? Because we are stronger when our faith roots interlock with others. Paul said, "Let your roots go down into him . . . then your faith will grow strong." Everyone looks fine in calm winds. But when the winds kick up, you had better have strong roots!

So, how deep do *your* roots go? Are you spending regular time with God? Are you securely connected with other believers? Here's what I can tell you from experience: the storms and high winds *will* come. It's just a matter of *when.* So prepare yourself. Take some steps that help your faith roots go deep into God. Spend top-quality time in His Word. Spend top-quality time with His people. Be as strong in your heart and your soul as you appear to be on the surface. Then when the winds come you'll be ready. And you'll stand tall when others fall. That's God's Word for you today.

> **Many people don't really make the effort to make their roots go deep in God.**

87

BE AN EPAPHRAS

Epaphras . . . always prays earnestly for you,
asking God to make you strong and perfect, fully
confident that you are following the whole will of God.
I can assure you that he prays hard for you.
(Colossians 4:12–13)

Do you have an "Epaphras"? Someone that you know who prays "earnestly" or "hard" for you? Some time ago I was hugging my congregation members after a worship service and one of them said something very moving to me. The person looked deeply into my eyes and said, "I pray every day for you." It literally brought tears to my eyes. I mean, I know I have people in my church who pray for me. Some pray that I will preach better. Some pray that I will preach shorter. Some pray that I'll let my associate pastor preach more often. Some may even be praying about where God may be calling me *next*. But this person was letting me know something special, something sacred, that each day this person was praying for *me*—not my preaching but *me*. It touched me more than the person will ever know.

I'm not sure exactly why that moment was so powerful for me. Maybe it's because I simply felt so utterly loved. I could tell this person's concern for me was sincere and deep. Maybe it's because as a pastor I'm used to doing all the caring for others and not so used to having others care for me. Maybe it's because I have such a deep respect for this person and that this person is someone whom I feel God truly listens to. Or maybe it's because I know how desperately I *need* those prayers. I need them for strength. I need them for wisdom. I need them for courage. I need those prayers for sensitivity to the Spirit of God. Whatever the reason, that encounter was inspiring, healing, and comforting to me. So when I read Paul's words to the Colossians about their friend Epaphras, I smiled. I imagine hearing that from Paul was as meaningful to them as hearing those words that day after church was to me.

I hope you have an Epaphras. Each of us needs one, which means we probably ought to *be* an Epaphras for someone as well! Who could use *your* prayers? To whom would it mean the world for you to say, "I pray for you every day," if they knew you really meant it? I know it would make someone's day to hear that from you. It sure made mine. You don't have to be a pastor, teacher, or leader in the church to be an Epaphras. You just have to be someone who cares deeply about someone else and believe in prayer enough to pray.

So go ahead. Find that person. Make a commitment to lift them up in prayer each day. Look deeply in the eyes of this person so they will see your love and know you're sincere. Then tell this person you pray for them every day. You'll melt the person's heart and make their day. And you'll become this person's Epaphras. That's God's Word for you today.

To whom would it mean the world for you to say,
"I pray for you every day"?

88

GOD'S UNWATED PROMISE

You know that we are destined for such troubles. Even while we were with you, we warned you that troubles would soon come—and they did, as you well know.
(1 Thessalonians 3:3–4)

Don't you love to claim the promises of God? We all do. We love to claim God's promise of peace. We love to claim God's promise of joy. We love to claim God's promise of victory.

But how about God's promise of *troubles*? Probably not so much. Is that really a promise? Absolutely. In John 16:33 Jesus said, "In this world you will have trouble" (NIV). Okay, maybe it's not so much a promise as it is simply a statement of reality. Either way, it's a truth we need to be prepared for.

That's the point Paul is making here to the Thessalonians, and it's an important one!

When we're not prepared for troubles on our faith journey, a few things happen. One, we will tend to take them personally. Many of us when bad stuff happens will say, "Why me?" rather than "Why *not* me?" We feel that we are somehow being singled out for troubles. But we're not. Troubles happen. When we're unprepared for troubles, we can also take too much responsibility for them. We feel that we must have done something wrong that *caused* these troubles.

But usually the cause is simply the fact that we live in a world where troubles are a part of the deal. We can also feel abandoned when troubles come and we're not prepared. It's hard to feel God when we're experiencing pain and panic. So it may seem to us as if He was there—but troubles came and now He's gone. But He's *not* gone. In fact, Psalm 34:18 reminds us that He is "close to the brokenhearted." In the midst of our troubles God is near—very near.

Maybe you're going through some troubles right now. Perhaps they caught you a bit off guard and you're struggling today. If so, let me help you regain some balance. It's not personal. Troubles happen to all of us. They happened to Jesus, they happened to Paul, and they've happened to me. It's just your turn.

You didn't cause these troubles to come your way either. So relax. God's not mad and getting back at you for something. And don't forget: God is *with* you. Right now, right here, in the midst of your troubles, God is with you. You are never, ever alone. If you're not going through troubles right now, reread today's passage again and just remind yourself.

Ready or not, troubles will be coming. Jesus promised they would. So did Paul. But don't be discouraged. Just prepare yourself by remembering what else Jesus said when He told us that troubles would happen: "Take heart! I have overcome the world" (NIV). Now *that's* a promise we *like* to claim! That's God's Word for you today.

It's hard to feel God when we're experiencing pain and panic.

89

FINDING GOD'S WILL

**Always be joyful. Never stop praying. Be thankful
in all circumstances, for this is God's will for
you who belong to Christ Jesus.
(1 Thessalonians 5:16–18)**

Many people talk to me about wanting to discover God's will for their lives. But what they really want, at least most of the time, is to know what decision will work out *perfectly* for them.

Somehow we have the mistaken idea that if this is the path God wants for me, then it'll be an easy one with little or no pain or difficulty. If that's true, then none of the disciples or Paul or even Jesus was following the path of God's will, because their paths were *hard*!

So can we know God's will? Sure we can. Paul gives it to us right here: "Always be joyful. Never stop praying. Be thankful in all circumstances, for this is God's will for you who belong to Christ Jesus." God's will is more about *how* you walk the path than it is about *which* path you walk.

"Should I buy this car or that car?" I believe God is a Toyota fan, but it probably doesn't matter to Him. Just be thankful that you *have* a car!

"Should I take this job or that job?" He may or may not care. But He does want you to be *joyful* on the job!

Obviously God doesn't want you to take paths or do things that violate His Word or character. But between those two guardrails, I believe His will is a lot broader than we think. I don't think God cares nearly as much about whether you become a nurse, a factory worker, or an engineer as He does about what *kind* of worker you are on those jobs. What's funny is that this is usually the part we focus the *least* on!

So are you following God's will for your life? Not "Have you found the 'perfect' mate or the 'perfect' job or the 'perfect' place to live?" But are you joyful? Are you prayerful? Are you thankful? Because regardless of whom you marry or where you work or live, that is the kind of person God desires you to be.

Please hear my heart. It's fine to pray about whom you should date, marry, or even be close friends with. It's good to pray about what vocation to choose and how your gifts might best be used. It's even a good idea to pray about where to live and about major changes you make.

But always remember that God is infinitely more concerned about the *kind of person* you are becoming than He is about your job or car or house. So go ahead and pray about the decisions you have to make. But pray even more about the kind of man or woman He wants you to be—because that's the heart of God's will for you! That's God's Word for you today.

God's will is more about **how** *you walk the path* *than it is about* **which** *path you walk.*

90

HOPE IS THE DIFFERENCE

*And now, dear brothers and sisters, we want you
to know what will happen to the believers who have died
so you will not grieve like people who have no hope. For
since we believe that Jesus died and was raised to life
again, we also believe that when Jesus returns, God will
bring back with him the believers who have died.*
(1 Thessalonians 4:13–14)

I was at a funeral this past Saturday for one of our
members. It's always sad when you say goodbye to
someone you care about. But the pastor leading the service
reminded us of something important: this man had lived
a good, long life and loved the Lord with all his heart. He
reminded us that we were there to *celebrate.*

The next day between worship services I spoke with a young man whose grandfather was near death. In fact, he was going to the hospital that afternoon where they were going to be removing his grandfather from life support. We talked for a bit, and then I prayed for him, that God would give him strength and peace. When I finished praying, he wiped the tears and said, "It's okay. We know where he's going." It was an assurance that somehow made the unbearable bearable.

In both of these experiences there was the presence of something that sets us apart as people of faith: *hope*. Even death can't take that from us.

Do you believe in life after death—I mean *really* believe? It makes a difference. It makes a difference in the way you live. Paul says it also makes a difference in the way you grieve. My observation is that it also makes a difference in the way you die. When you're confident of life with God beyond the grave, you don't dread death. You don't necessarily *want* it to happen, but you don't live in frantic fear of it. You're more nervous about the process of dying than the end result.

What I can tell you, particularly about people who are older and are people of faith, is that they come to a place at which they're *ready* for death. Heaven isn't a myth to them—it's a reality. They believe with all their hearts that God and many of the ones they love are waiting for them. And they are ready to join them. Paul confirms that thought.

Sometimes, especially during holidays and special occasions, we really miss those we love who have died. It's hard to celebrate when they aren't here to join us. That's natural. But maybe it'll help to remind ourselves that if our loved ones were believers, our sadness is really for us, not them. They truly are in a better place. They don't hurt anymore. They don't suffer anymore. They are freed from all the plagues and problems we call "life." My guess is they are a bit sad for us! They know that if we really knew what eternity was like, we'd probably be jealous of them, or we would at least be happy that they are getting to enjoy such an incredible experience.

So shed a tear for yourself if it helps you. But give a smile toward heaven for those you miss, because they are now filled with total joy. And hold on to that one thing that truly makes us different from those who don't believe: hope. That's God's Word for you today.

Do you believe in life after death—
I mean **really** *believe? It makes a difference.*

91

YOU, ME, AND JEFFREY DAHMER

This is a trustworthy saying, and everyone should accept it: "Christ Jesus came into the world to save sinners"—and I am the worst of them all. But God had mercy on me so that Christ Jesus could use me as a prime example of his great patience with even the worst sinners. Then others will realize that they, too, can believe in him and receive eternal life.
(1 Timothy 1:15–16)

A few years ago at a men's conference I gave a message titled "The Gospel According to Jeffrey Dahmer." Many of you will recall that Jeffrey Dahmer raped, murdered, and dismembered seventeen boys and men in the Milwaukee area between 1978 and 1991. He even cannibalized some of them.

At the beginning of the message I showed a YouTube video of Dahmer being interviewed in prison. In that video he talks about growing up believing that there was no God, leading him to believe he wasn't accountable to anyone. He felt as if he were his own god.

But while Dahmer was in prison, a pastor reached out to him. Over a period of time and through a lot of conversation, Jeffrey Dahmer claimed to have come to faith in Christ. The interview, recorded just months before Dahmer was killed in prison, was riveting. Though many might say conversions in prison can't be trusted, he sounded sincere.

So what do *you* think? Can a murderer like that really come to faith? Is it possible for someone that vile to be forgiven?

According to Paul, yes, they can. Paul himself had been a murderer. He had been a leader among a group who tracked down early Christians and had them put to death. He had taken families from their homes. He had taken parents from their children. He had people stoned to death for no more a crime than saying that they believed Jesus was the Messiah, God in the flesh.

Then one day Paul had a conversion experience. He encountered Jesus in an amazing and powerful way. And this zealous persecutor of Christians became a Christ follower himself. Not only that, but he also became a preacher and church planter! His words to Timothy were basically "If God can save me, He can save *anyone*"—maybe even Jeffrey Dahmer.

Paul's words should also give you hope today. If you've had a rather dark past and have done things you know to be horribly wrong, God's grace is great enough for you too. No matter how many times the enemy reminds you of your sins or how awful they were, God has it covered. You can fully and completely rest in that. It should also give you hope for the people in your world you feel are just too far gone.

They're not. If God can redeem the calloused heart of a murderer like Paul, He can redeem them too. There is no "bottom" to the depth of God's grace. Paul contended that if it was deep enough for him, it's deep enough for anyone. And that includes you, me, and Jeffrey Dahmer. That's God's Word for you today.

> *No matter how many times the enemy reminds you of your sins, God has it covered.*

92

THE GREATEST MISSION FIELD
IS IN YOUR LAP

*I remember your genuine faith, for you share
the faith that first filled your grandmother Lois
and your mother, Eunice. And I know that same
faith continues strong in you.*
(2 Timothy 1:5)

Reading today's verse brought back to me fond memories of my grandmother. We called her "Mom," and she was influential in my faith development, just as Timothy's grandmother was for him.

Mom was one of those kind souls who always made me feel special and loved. She was also one of the people in my life who felt that God had something special for me. When I told her I was going to college to get a degree in ministry, she said, "I always knew you'd make a preacher!" While I was in school, she would send me $5 in an envelope every couple of weeks or so just to make sure I had some money. She would fawn all over me when I came home to visit and was extremely proud when I got my first ministry position. When she died in 1997 I had the privilege of preaching her funeral. I also sang the song "Thank You" for the role she played in my life.

As I stood by her casket for the last time before they closed it, I placed one of my business cards inside. I put my hand on hers and said, "Thank you for believing in me, Mom. I made it. I'm a preacher." It was a sacred moment for me.

Never underestimate the role you play in the development of faith in your children and grandchildren. From the very beginning of time, God ordained that the *family* would be His primary vehicle of passing the faith from one generation to the next. Churches, Christian schools, and other believers will also certainly play a part, but there is an imprint of faith that a parent or grandparent can leave that is like no other.

Paul was careful to point out to Timothy where the roots of his faith came from. Perhaps it was because he wanted him to know he had been given a sacred trust that was to be protected, developed, and maximized. Or maybe it was because he wanted Timothy to know that it was now *his turn* to plant the seeds of faith in his own children. Even though Timothy was now a pastor and church planter, there would be no more important mission field than the one in his own home.

The same is true for us. Not all of us get to be pastors or church planters. But *all* of us who are parents and grandparents can leave spiritual imprints on the next generation. It may be our encouragement and sharing our stories of faith. It may be reading Bible storybooks to them when they're young. It may be taking them to church with us. It may be calling out the things of God we see in them as my grandmother did for me. You don't have to be a spiritual giant to make an impact with them. Your love for them and the love they have for you make their hearts and spirits fertile ground in which to plant God's seeds.

Don't miss your chance to pass your faith along. The greatest mission field God has for you may be sitting right there in your lap. You may be holding the next Timothy or Steve. So love them well and let your light shine before them. You may be the spark of faith that helps them set the world on fire for God! That's God's Word for you today.

All of us who are parents and grandparents can leave spiritual imprints on the next generation.

93

TOUGH LOVE FOR TOXIC PEOPLE

If people are causing divisions among you,
give a first and second warning. After that, have
nothing more to do with them.
(Titus 3:10)

There are some people you need to live without. I know—that doesn't sound like a very "Christian" thing to say. But it's true. There are people who are simply toxic. Maybe they don't know any better. Maybe they don't realize how much chaos and pain their influence causes. Maybe they have been hurt deeply themselves and they simply vent that hurt by causing pain and problems for other people.

But it doesn't matter—if they continually cause problems, create divisions, and make life miserable, you're better off without them. That's what Paul is getting at here. Toxic people need to be confronted. They need to know that their divisiveness is hurtful and unacceptable. If they are reasonable people and their hearts are good, they will stop. But sometimes people feel they have a "right" to do or say whatever they want to whomever they want. That's when they need us to draw the boundaries for them.

I've seen churches stuck and unable to move forward in their ministry and mission all because there is one toxic person whom no one has the guts to stand up to. Many of these churches eventually shrink to a size where they are unable to continue existing. I've seen families who have allowed an obnoxious, controlling, or demanding family member ruin almost every single gathering because they don't have the courage to call them out and say, "Enough is enough." Eventually family members start making up excuses not to come, and relationships between healthy members of the family are lost because no one wants to stop the unhealthy one.

I've seen businesses and organizations that can't keep good employees because there's a toxic manager or employee who makes the work culture so unhealthy that good people don't want to be a part of it. But rather than confront them, change them, or fire them, the manager or owner just lets it go on. And then they wonder why turnover at their company is so high.

As a classic codependent, I know how difficult it is to have confrontational conversations with divisive people. But I've learned the hard way that if you don't deal with toxic people, you default the leadership of your family, your church, or your job to them. You let *their* disease drive *your* life! I believe our mission as a church, our intimacy as a family, and our culture where we work are just too important to allow that. I hope you do to.

So if you have a toxic person who seems bent on running and ruining your life and relationships, warn them—even twice. But after that, draw whatever boundaries you need in order to keep yourself, your church, and your job healthy, safe, and sane. If you feel guilty as you draw those hard lines, just remind yourself that you are acting with the love of Jesus. Because sometimes the kind of Jesus love people need is tough love. And sometimes *you* have to be the one to dispense it! That's God's Word for you today.

Toxic people need to be confronted. They need to know that their divisiveness is hurtful and unacceptable.

94

LOVE **DOES**

I always thank my God when I pray for you,
Philemon, because I keep hearing about your faith
in the Lord Jesus and your love for all of God's
people. And I am praying that you will put into
action the generosity that comes from your faith as
you understand and experience all the good
things we have in Christ.
(Philemon 1:4–6)

Love *does*. It doesn't just feel—it does. It doesn't just care—it does. It doesn't just hope—it does.

That's a message we all need to hear. We often think of ourselves as being "loving" people. But somewhere along the way we have to understand that love is *behavior* and not just intention or emotion. If a person is truly a loving individual, it will display itself in how they speak, act, and what they do.

You have to love how Paul put Philemon on the spot by saying, "I keep *hearing* about your faith . . . and love . . . and I am praying the you will *put into action* the generosity that comes from your faith" (vv. 5–6, emphasis added). In other words, "Is this talk about your being so loving just hearsay or is there action that you're going to put with that?" Ouch!

Paul was sending a former slave named Onesimus back to Philemon. For some reason their relationship had been severed. From the text it seems that maybe Onesimus had not been doing his job well. Perhaps he had even been lazy. Somehow he ended up with Paul.

But now he had become a Christ follower, and with it he had a different work ethic. Paul's question to Philemon is "Can you forgive him and give him a second chance?" It's a great question. It's easy to *say* you'll forgive. It's a lot harder to actually do the hard work of trusting someone enough to give the person their position back. That's love *doing*. Paul is challenging Philemon to live up to his reputation by putting forgiveness into action. Because love *does*.

So where do you need to put love into action? Do you simply say you love, or does it show? Does it come out in the way you speak to others? Does it come out in demonstrations of kindness? Does your love pour out of you in acts of generosity and sacrifice? Does your love express itself in the way you are willing to forgive by offering a second chance?

A lot of people care. Many are compassionate. Some even say they are forgiving. But let your love be more than that. Let your love be a love that is more than just words or feelings or intentions. Let your love be known by its action. Because love *does*! That's God's Word for you today.

> *We have to understand that love is **behavior** and not just intention or emotion.*

95

JESUS HAS BEEN THERE

This High Priest of ours understands our weaknesses, for he faced all of the same testings we do, yet he did not sin. So let us come boldly to the throne of our gracious God. There we will receive his mercy, and we will find grace to help us when we need it most.
(Hebrews 4:15–16)

A few years ago a fitness trainer named Drew Manning did something really wild. He grew weary of his clients complaining about how hard it was for them to change their eating habits and work out to lose weight. So he decided to show them just how easy it actually is. For six months he stopped working out and ate the way his clients did—chips, sodas, greasy burgers, the whole nine yards.

His chiseled physique began to sag and bulge. He gained seventy pounds! Then he went back to his healthful ways—clean eating, lots of water, and steady exercise. Little by little the old Drew came back. It took him a full six months to get back to where he had been before.

But something else happened for him: *empathy.* He admitted to his clients that it was a lot harder getting back into shape than he imagined. His body craved the fat and the sugar once he stopped eating it. Pushing his out-of-shape body to exercise took more energy and motivation than he thought it would.

Manning once more looked the way a fitness trainer was supposed to look, but he was changed on the inside. Now he was more patient and encouraging with his clients because he saw them with different eyes. He *knew* what they were going through. He had felt their pain and suffering.

We have a spiritual trainer like that. Jesus has more than compassion for us—He has *empathy* as well. He felt what we feel. He knows what it's like to feel pain. He knows the sting of betrayal and the grief of loss. He knows what it's like to be cold and hungry and to be misunderstood and falsely accused. All those temptations you wrestle with? Yes, He dealt with them too. When you come to Him in prayer, you are not talking to someone who shakes His head at your whining. He *gets* it. He not only listens to us with a gracious heart—He listens with an *understanding* heart. He came from heaven to earth to put Himself through the grueling, enduring struggle that we call "life." He even went through the fearful passage we call "death." From the beginning of our struggles to the end, He understands.

So as you pray today, don't be afraid to open your heart. You're not talking to a judgmental God. You're talking to a God who *gets* you. He knows what you're feeling and He knows what you're facing. He has walked in your shoes and lived in your skin. He doesn't just see what you're going through—He went through it Himself.

So put the full weight of your struggle on the table before Jesus. He's not just a wonderful priest who is willing to listen to your troubles. He's an understanding priest who has *lived* in your troubles! He's an empathetic friend who has "been there." And because He's been there, He can truly be *here.* That's God's Word for you today.

> **Jesus is an understanding Priest who has lived in your troubles.**

96

TREAT THEM *ALL* LIKE ANGELS!

Don't forget to show hospitality to strangers,
for some who have done this have entertained
angels without realizing it!
(Hebrews 13:2)

In April 2015 a man named Mike walked into a restaurant in New York City. As he ordered his meal he was impressed with his waitress. She was pleasant, attentive, and in his words, "humble." They engaged in conversation as she served him. She asked about what he did and seemed to be genuinely interested and encouraging.

As he inquired into her life, one of the discoveries he made was that she had recently been served with an eviction notice. It broke his heart to think that someone as sweet as her had to struggle as she did. When he got his bill for his meal, it was $43.50. He thought about her situation and decided to take the advice of his old middle school teacher who had challenged his class to "pay it forward" whenever they got a chance to do something kind. So he decided to give her a nice tip: a $3,000 tip! She was obviously blown away by his kindness. On the back of the bill he wrote her a nice note of encouragement. It was a night she'll never forget.

Let's rewind the tape a bit to the beginning of the story. When the man came in and was seated in her area of service, do you think she had any idea that he was capable of such an act of kindness? Of course not. Tips like that have happened to only a handful of servers across the years. But she *treated* him as if he were capable of such a tip. My guess is that she treated all of her customers as if they were capable of such a tip. She didn't do it so she could one day cash in. She did it because she believed that people deserved to be treated that way, even though her life was extremely stressful and difficult. And one day she served an angel of a guy who gave her a gift in response to her kind service that was beyond anything she could imagine.

The Hebrews writer reminds us that we never know when that next stranger we meet might actually be an angel. Don't miss his point. Treat *everyone* as if they're an angel. But don't do it because you hope for an angel-size tip, a gift, or some kind of divine blessing in return. Do it because every single person you meet is worthy of being treated that way. Each person you meet is someone who was created in the image of God, made "just a little lower than the angels" (Hebrews 2:7). There is a piece of God in every one of them. So they are deserving of being treated with dignity and kindness, even the ones who have buried that piece of God so deeply it rarely shows.

If nothing else, treat them like angels because *you* are an "angel." Because even if you never end up with a $3,000 tip, you're treating them how *you* would like to be treated. And you bring great joy to your Father when you live that way. That's God's Word for you today.

> *There is a piece of God in every single person you meet.*

97

GOOGLE AND GOD

If you need wisdom, ask our generous God,
and he will give it to you. He will not rebuke you for
asking. But when you ask him, be sure that your
faith is in God alone. Do not waver, for a person
with divided loyalty is as unsettled as a wave of the
sea that is blown and tossed by the wind.
(James 1:5–6)

My grandson got a Google Home Mini for Christmas. It's one of those devices to which you ask questions and it gives you the answers. We were having some fun with it by asking it different kinds of things. My son asked it a physics question and it gave him the answer. We asked it about the weather in France and it told us. We asked if it was going to snow in Oklahoma City tonight and it assured us it was not. We asked what the original thirteen colonies were, and it told us. It's actually a pretty handy little device.

But every once in a while we would ask it a question that it didn't know, and it would say, "I don't know the answer to that—I'm still learning." You have to realize its limitations. What Google can give you is *information*. It can access millions and millions of facts. What it can't give you is *wisdom*. And wisdom is what most of us really need!

James reminds us that that's where God comes in. God can give us more than facts. He can give us *guidance*. He can give us *direction*. God can help us look at the decisions we are facing and give us *discernment*. He can help us find the best path for our future. God is more than smart—He is *wise*.

But there is a caveat with it: we have to actually listen and heed His advice! Many times after we've prayed for wisdom and God gives it, we decide it's not the advice we really wanted—so we seek a second opinion. We may even seek three or four other opinions, usually with the hope of finding someone who will tell us to do what we've wanted to do all along. You see, the down side of seeking wisdom from God is that He's going to tell us the truth. And in the famous words of Jack Nicholson, some of us can't handle the truth.

So if you just want information today, ask Google. It can quote you facts from history and tell you all kinds of interesting things about what humanity has learned.

But if you need *wisdom*, ask God. He can help you with direction in your life, your home, and your future. Just make sure you ask Him with an open mind and an obedient heart. Because all the wisdom in the world is useless if you don't follow it. That's God's Word for you today.

Many times after we've prayed for wisdom and God gives it, we decide it's not the advice we really wanted—so we seek a second opinion.

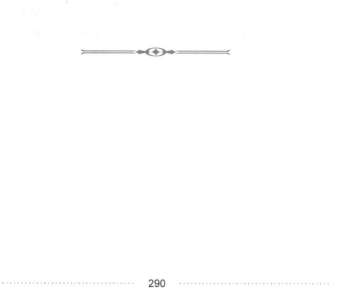

98

THE HIGHER, HARDER ROAD

God called you to do good, even if it means
suffering, just as Christ suffered for you. He is your
example, and you must follow in his steps.
(1 Peter 2:21)

I was reading not long ago about a pastor in another country who was jailed for preaching the gospel. The conditions of the prison were horrible. But when the pastor had a chance to speak to some of his friends, he told them not to pray for his release. He told them instead to pray for him to represent Jesus well while he was in jail. He was not nearly as concerned for his safety or even his release as he was about representing Christ in an uplifting way.

So he didn't ask his friends to plead for his freedom. He didn't ask them to try to fight for better treatment for him while he was behind bars. He didn't even ask them to try to secure the best lawyer to represent him in court. He asked for prayers to be the best he could be in that horrible and unjust place. He asked them to pray that he would be like Jesus.

Can I be honest with you? That's a whole other level of godliness that I am nowhere close to yet. It's not that I don't try following the example of Jesus. I do, of course. But the example I try to follow is the one of striving to be kind, seeking to be helpful, listening to others, and working to be sensitive to what they're going through. You know what I mean? I try to be *nice* like Jesus.

But what Peter is talking about here is beyond that. It's choosing the high road even when you're being treated unfairly. It's choosing not to retaliate when someone has hurt you. It's choosing not to get back at someone who has wronged you. It's choosing to embrace the "suffering" moments as the *best* moments to be like Jesus rather than justifying those times as moments when we don't have to. It's a harder and higher road that most of us don't even *try* to attain. But Peter tells us that when we follow Jesus, that higher and harder road of suffering is where His footsteps lead.

So if you're suffering a bit unfairly right now, don't take it as an offense. Take it as an opportunity. If you say you follow Jesus, look at this as just a little higher and harder road than you've had to walk so far. I'm not saying you have to *like* the suffering. I'm just saying that following Jesus is more than just being a "nice" person in convenient times to deserving people.

Jesus was *perfect* and He was treated horribly anyway. And even though He could have retaliated in powerful and dramatic ways, He didn't. He chose the higher and harder road of love—*real* love, lay-your-life-down kind of love. Not many are able to walk that high a road. Are you? That's God's Word for you today.

It's choosing to embrace the "suffering" moments as the* best *moments to be like Jesus.

99

NO GOOD GUYS AND BAD GUYS

If we claim we have no sin, we are only fooling ourselves and not living in the truth. But if we confess our sins to him, he is faithful and just to forgive us our sins and to cleanse us from all wickedness.
(1 John 1:8–9)

This two-verse passage is one of my favorites in the Bible. It reminds me of three very important truths. The first truth is "I am no better than anyone else." That's an important fact to never forget. It means simply this: We are *all* sinners.

Sometimes when I look at some of horrible things people do, I am appalled. I shake my head and wonder how in the world people can be so evil and do such wicked stuff. But then when I look in the mirror of my own soul, I'm reminded that I'm no better. I've never killed, but I've wished a few people dead. I've never stolen, but I've certainly envied. I've never blasphemed God, but I've not always lived up to His name either. As much as I want to excuse myself and say I'm not as bad as "those guys," the reality is that I'm not without sin. If pride, anger, and jealousy are sin, then I'm guilty as charged. And I need to be reminded of that once in a while.

But this passage also reminds me that I'm not any *worse* than anyone else. When you have a strong streak of shame inside you as I do, you need to remember that truth as well. Have you ever felt as if you were the worst person in the whole world? If so, you probably have that curse of shame yourself. But you're not worse than anyone else. And neither am I. We're all just as bad. We're *all* sinners. All these people you have on a pedestal, believing they don't wrestle with stuff like you do? They're sinners too. John says if they say they're not, they're liars. And since lying is a sin, that makes them sinners for sure!

But the *great news* of this passage is the third truth. And that truth is that not only is there a level ground of sin, but there is also an equal opportunity for forgiveness. John reminds us that no matter who we are or what we've done, when we confess our sin to God, He is willing to forgive us of that sin. Whether it's sin of the heart, sin of attitude, or sin of behavior, it's all wiped away by God's grace when we confess. It's a done deal, paid in full, gone.

So don't wallow in your pride that you're above all those other "sinners." You're not. You are just as bad. And don't wallow in your shame either. You're not any worse. Just confess your sin to God. Then you'll discover what we all have to learn. This is not a world of good guys and bad guys. It's a whole world of bad guys who can all be *made* good the same way—by the incredible grace of our Lord Jesus Christ! That's God's Word for you today.

> *This is not a world of good guys and bad guys.*
> *It's a whole world of bad guys who can all be*
> **made** *good the same way!*

100

WHEN ALL OUR DIFFERENCES FADE AWAY

*From the throne came a voice that said,
"Praise our God, all his servants, all who fear him,
from the least to the greatest." Then I heard again what
sounded like the shout of a vast crowd or the roar
of mighty ocean waves or the crash of loud thunder:
"Praise the Lord! For the Lord our
God, the Almighty, reigns."*
(Revelation 19:5–6)

Several years ago I had the privilege of speaking at a conference in Grand Cayman in the Cayman Islands. It was an incredible week of enjoying life on the island and exploring a part of the world I had not been in before. The crystal-clear water, snorkeling among the exotic fish, letting the stingrays brush up against us in Stingray City, the island food—it was all simply incredible.

But the highlight of the week for me was the final worship service that Sunday. All the churches came together for the service, and the music was amazing! They were passionate and energetic, which is the only way islanders know how to worship.

But it was sharing Communion that really got me. I watched as all these people came forward, representing dozens of different nationalities from all around the world, participating together. They were young and old. Some were dressed to the nines and others were in shorts and flowered shirts. They spoke different languages and came from different backgrounds. Some were wealthy and some quite poor. But they were all taking the cup and bread together. As the tears rolled down my face, all I could think about was "This must be what heaven is going to be like." I think our passage today confirms that.

If you struggle with people who are different from you, heaven may come as quite a shock when you arrive. Because many will be there—people of all colors; people from all kinds of backgrounds; people who like to be loud when they worship, raising their hands and clapping and dancing;

people who are quiet in worship, with heads bowed and tears flowing. There will be people there who had an opposite political point of view from you here on earth. There will be people who had a different theological view. There will be people there who you will probably be shocked to see. There will be people there who will probably be shocked to see *you*! It will be a crowd of every kind of background, nationality, and perspective you can imagine. But none of that will matter. We'll hardly even notice one another. All eyes will be on The Throne. All our differences will fade away in the brilliance of our Almighty God.

In heaven we'll finally understand that we all got there the same way—by the grace of our Lord Jesus Christ. The Lamb who was slain was slain for *all* of us. We will all wear the glorious robes that shine with His glory. In heaven there will be no "insiders" and "outsiders." We are all family. God made us all His children with One Father and One Big Brother, Jesus.

So you might rethink all those walls you're building and all those people you find yourself looking down your nose at. One day you may find yourself shoulder-to-shoulder with those people, singing praise songs to God in heaven. They are a lot more like you than you know.

One day none of these cosmetic differences will matter anyway. All that will matter will be The One who got us all there. And together we'll sing, "Our God reigns!" That's God's Word for you today.

In heaven we'll finally understand that we all got there the same way— by the grace of our Lord Jesus Christ.

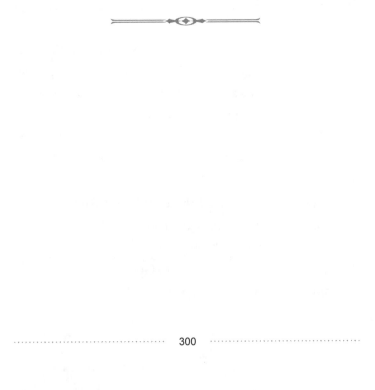

ABOUT THE AUTHOR

Steve Chiles is senior pastor of the Shartel Church of God in Oklahoma City. He is a graduate of Mid-America Christian University and has served in ministry for thirty-eight years as a pastor, a church consultant, and a ministry coach to pastors. Steve is a frequent speaker and conference leader for conventions, leadership development workshops, men's retreats, and other special events. He is a dynamic communicator with a gifted ability to inspire and challenge. He has written for several Christian magazines and other publications and writes a daily devotional titled "God's Word for You Today." In his free time Steve enjoys working out, golfing, viewing movies, and is a huge fan of the Oklahoma City Thunder. Steve's wife, Wanda, is a licensed counselor. The couple has two grown sons and two *amazing* grandchildren!